SACRED
singleness

LESLIE LUDY

HARVEST HOUSE PUBLISHERS
EUGENE, OREGON

Unless otherwise indicated, all verses are taken from the New King James Version. Copyright © 1982 by Thomas Nelson, Inc. Used by permission. All rights reserved.

Verses marked KJV are taken from the King James Version of the Bible.

Verses marked NASB are taken from the New American Standard Bible®, © 1960, 1962, 1963, 1968, 1971, 1972, 1973, 1975, 1977, 1995 by The Lockman Foundation. Used by permission. (www .Lockman.org)

Verses marked NIV are taken from the HOLY BIBLE, NEW INTERNATIONAL VERSION®. NIV®. Copyright © 1973, 1978, 1984 by the International Bible Society. Used by permission of Zondervan. All rights reserved.

Verses marked ESV are from The Holy Bible, English Standard Version, copyright © 2001 by Crossway Bibles, a division of Good News Publishers. Used by permission. All rights reserved.

Verses marked YOUNG'S are taken from the Young's literal translation of the Bible.

Cover by Abris, Veneta, Oregon

Cover photo © Senthil Kumar / Comet Photography / Corbis

Published in association with Loyal Arts Literary Agency, LoyalArts.com

SACRED SINGLENESS
Copyright © 2009 by Winston and Brooks, Inc.
Published by Harvest House Publishers
Eugene, Oregon 97402
www.harvesthousepublishers.com

Library of Congress Cataloging-in-Publication Data
    Ludy, Leslie.
    Sacred singleness / Leslie Ludy.
        p. cm.
    ISBN 978-0-7369-2288-3 (pbk.)
    ISBN 978-0-7369-3463-3 (eBook)
    1. Single women—Religious life. 2. Christian women—Religious life. I. Title.
    BV4596.S5L84 2009
    248.8'432—dc22
                                        2008049429

Printed in the United States of America

12 13 14 15 16 17 / VP-SK / 10 9 8 7 6 5

Contents

Part Three
Living a Poured-Out Life
A Sacred Season Awaits!

Author's Note

When I first began contemplating writing a book on singleness, I felt a little nervous. After all, my own season of singleness was relatively short, which might seem to disqualify me from this subject. For the past 14 years, Eric and I have spoken to countless thousands of unmarried young people about God's plan for this season of their lives, and along the way I've encountered plenty of single young women who look at me with a fishy eye. The vibe I get from them is, "Don't talk to me about being content with my singleness, honey, while you are happily married!"

I understand their chagrin. I mean, you wouldn't want someone who has never driven a car giving you pointers on how to operate a motor vehicle. Or someone who has never used a stove giving you tips on the best way to fry an egg. But this is not merely a book about my own singleness experience. And it's not a book in which I flippantly declare, "All you single young women out there should stop complaining about how hard it is to be single!" (as I sit here blissfully married).

Rather, this book is about laying down your life for Jesus Christ; surrendering every hope, dream, desire, and ambition to Him. Exchanging your own agenda for His. Awakening to His glorious purpose for this sacred season of your life. It's a message about the true Gospel.

And *that* is a subject I understand quite well—both through personal experience and through interacting with thousands of young women for the past 14 years. I have found that single young women typically fall into one of two categories: those who are consumed with their own desires, and are discontented and unfulfilled in their singleness, and those who are consumed by a passionate romance with Jesus Christ, and are radiantly and joyfully pouring out their lives for Him. It is my hope and prayer that this book will equip you to be among the latter; to discover the amazing opportunity, unmatched joy, and abundant life that awaits every fully surrendered young woman. Because this world is in desperate need of young women who are willing to take up their cross and follow their King.

Modern Christian culture has been flooded with messages that sell the true Gospel short. It's not about becoming a living sacrifice for Christ anymore; it's about finding your heart's desires and living your best life. The area of singleness and marriage has been no exception. We've been trying to glean all the benefits of Christ while avoiding the cross. This book takes a stand against that kind of self-focused Christianity. It's not just a book about finding fulfillment in your singleness. It's a book about applying the Gospel of Jesus Christ to your singleness. It's not an easy message, but it's a glorious one.

In the pages of this book I candidly share the journey God took me on as a single young woman, and the truths He has continued to teach me about a fully surrendered life as a married young woman. These are timeless truths that I believe can radically impact you, no matter what season of life you are in. In addition, I've included many firsthand stories and testimonials of modern-day single young women who are living radiant, joyful, Christ-consumed lives and being mightily used for the kingdom of God. They are everyday young women who struggle with loneliness and personal desires just like you and me—and yet they have allowed the amazing power of Christ to turn their challenges into triumphs. I believe you will be inspired, uplifted, and encouraged by their examples. There is also a bonus interview with Krissy, my amazing sister-in-law, who, in case you haven't read any of my other books, is a veteran at radiant, Christ-centered singleness!

It is my hope that the message of this book will awaken you to the incredible plans and purposes God has for this solo season of your life—whether you are 17 or 57. He sees your every heart's desire. He knows your every fear. And He is waiting to meet your every need and make your life into a beautiful display of His glory, starting today.

Part One

First Love

A Romance with the One Who Fills All In All

1

Forsaking All
My Story of Surrender

...the fullness of Him who fills all in all.
EPHESIANS 1:23

*God has made us for Himself, and our hearts can never know
rest and perfect satisfaction until they find it in Him.*
HANNAH HURNARD

His name was Kyle.

He was a perfectly nice guy. Attractive, clean-cut, polite, moral. An upstanding "Christian" guy who went to church and believed in saving sex until marriage. The kind of guy my youth pastors and parents approved of.

Kyle liked me. I wasn't really enamored with him, but I was lonely. I hadn't had a boyfriend in about a year, and I was beginning to feel insecure and impatient. I loathed being single. I hated the stigma of not having someone in my life. It made me feel ugly and second rate. Not having a guy in my life was like being the kid on the playground who didn't get picked for the dodgeball team—alone, rejected, and overlooked.

So after three rather shallow conversations, Kyle became my boyfriend. We started talking on the phone every night, going out to dinner a few times a week, meeting for coffee on weekends, holding hands, sweetly kissing each other good night. It was all very innocent. We even talked about God. We went to church and Bible studies together and discussed what we were learning.

On the outside, it looked like a great Christian relationship—healthy, pure, and Christ centered. But in reality the only reason Kyle was in my life was because of my loneliness and insecurity.

I knew that a romance with Kyle wasn't God's highest for me. Kyle didn't lead me closer to Jesus Christ. Sure, he talked about God and did all the right "Christian" activities. He didn't smoke, cuss, drink, or have premarital sex. But selfishness was at the core of Kyle's existence. He didn't live for God's glory—he lived for his own agenda. Christianity was just an afterthought to him—not the primary purpose of his existence. He wasn't a bond servant of Jesus Christ. He was simply a churchgoer, enslaved to his own whims and desires. Kyle didn't wake up each morning thinking, *How can I love, serve, and honor Jesus Christ today?* Rather, his attitude was, *How can I serve my own agenda today, and still somehow stay within proper Christian boundaries?*

Truth be told, I didn't want to end up with a guy like Kyle. I longed for a valiant and noble hero—a gallant knight who would sweep me off my feet and cherish me as his princess forever. I wanted a truly Christlike man; a man who was intensely passionate for God, a man who was willing even to spill his own blood to bring glory to the name of Jesus. I had read about great men—men like Jim Elliot, Hudson Taylor, and John Wesley. Their version of masculinity caused my feminine heart to stand up and applaud. I desired to be with a man who would go to all lengths for his Lord; a man who's life would inspire others to take up their cross daily for the sake of the Gospel.

The problem was, it didn't seem that men like this existed anymore. Moral-but-mediocre guys like Kyle seemed to be the cream of the crop. His version of manhood looked pretty good next to the scores of perverted, debased, and arrogant males I met on a daily basis. After years of encountering the warped masculinity of my generation, I had come to believe that finding a semi-decent guy like Kyle was probably the best I could hope for. True, he wasn't the heroic Christlike gentleman I'd always dreamed of, but at least he was nice, went to church, and didn't pressure me to have sex with him.

So I settled.

The longer Kyle was in my life, the more I began to feel a pressure upon my soul. It was as if God was whispering, "This relationship isn't My best for your life, Leslie. Are you willing to let Me become your all in all instead of always trying to cure your loneliness with a guy?"

The question terrified me.

I had grown up in church singing songs about Jesus being my all in all—how He was everything I needed, the One who fulfilled the cry of my heart every day. But if I were to be honest, I had to admit that it was all just good-sounding Christian jargon to say those things. I didn't *really* believe that Jesus Christ could actually satisfy my heart at the deepest level and *actually be* my all in all. The truth was that I didn't really think I could be happy, fulfilled, and content without having a guy to turn to for comfort. And I couldn't imagine feeling confident and secure without having a boyfriend at my side to stroke my ego.

Like most girls my age, I was merely *enduring* these years as a single young woman. I spent most of my energy pining for the day when I would finally meet "the one," walk down the aisle in a white dress, and live happily ever after in a cute little house with a flower garden and white picket fence. *When I finally get married, that's when I will truly be happy and fulfilled*, I told myself subconsciously. I was convinced that when I finally shed the "curse of singleness," my dreams would come true and my life would finally have real meaning and purpose.

I was so repulsed by the thought of spending life alone, of never having my dreams of earthly romance come true, that I was willing to settle for a less-than-Christlike guy in order to avoid being single.

This is the plight of nearly every single young woman I've encountered over the last 14 years. We want to be fully set apart for Christ. We want Him to be our all in all. We want to find our fulfillment and satisfaction in Him, even if an earthly romance never comes our way.

But all too often, these desires are nothing more than good Christian sentiments that quickly fall by the wayside as soon as a semi-decent guy comes along. The moment we see an opportunity to shed the stigma of singleness, we cave. Instead of allowing Jesus Christ to be our first love, we look to earthly guys to meet needs in our heart that only Jesus Christ can fulfill. And we end up disappointed and dissatisfied...time and time again.

Don't get me wrong—I believe God is very interested in marriage. He doesn't call all of us to be single. In fact, for the large majority of us, He wants to script a beautiful lifelong earthly romance that will bring Him glory and be a reflection of heaven on earth.

But here is the crucial truth that all too many of us miss in our quest for true love: Even a beautiful God-scripted love story can never satisfy the way Jesus does. Even the most heroic and Christlike man on earth can never fulfill the longings of our heart like the true Prince and Lover of our soul. And until we are able to *truly* make Him our first love, until we are willing to give up our dream of an earthly love story for His sake, we will never know the fullness of Him who fills us all in all. We will always be looking to a mere man to meet the desires of our heart, rather than to the One who created us, who knows us better than we know ourselves, and who gave His very life's blood to rescue us.

Jesus said, "If anyone comes to Me and does not hate his father and mother, wife and children, brothers and sisters, yes, and his own life also, he cannot be My disciple...whoever of you does not forsake all that he has cannot be My disciple" (Luke 14:26,33).

As a single young woman, these words of Christ were not the reality of my life. As much as I hated to admit it, I had been clinging to my dream of an earthly love story and letting it take first place in my heart, even above Jesus Christ—the Prince of heaven and earth—who gave His life to set me free. I was so concerned with my own happiness, so consumed with my own fairy-tale ideal, that I had forsaken my first love.

Long before God wrote my love story with Eric, He wrote a different love story for me—a love story far more important and significant. It was the greatest love story of all time—a daily romance with the One who had given His very life to rescue me. And He was asking me to put *that* love story first, far above my desire for human companionship.

He wanted me to lay down my "right" to be married, walk down the aisle in a white dress, and live in a cute house with a white picket fence. He was asking me to let Him be everything to me, to satisfy every need, longing, and desire in my heart—even if an earthly prince never came my way.

It was the greatest challenge I had ever faced. Could I really let go of my precious dreams? Could I really lay my lifelong fairy-tale desires at the foot of His cross? What if He never gave them back? Would He really be enough to fulfill the desires of my heart, even if I never got married?

The great preacher Paris Reidhead once said, "Is not the Lamb who was slain worthy of the reward of His suffering?" That was the question my Lord was pressing upon my heart. Was not the One who had given everything for me worthy of everything I could offer Him?

My heroes are women throughout history who were willing to lay down their lives for the glory of Jesus Christ; women like Gladys Aylward, who left home and family at the age of 26 and spent the rest of her life spilling herself out for the poor and least in war-torn China; women like Jackie Pullinger, who from the age of 20 shared her home with drug addicts and prostitutes in the filthy Walled City of Hong Kong; women like Amy Carmichael, who gave up wealth and comforts at the age of 28 and gave her life for the exploited children of India. Many of the amazing Christian women of history never got married. When they laid everything down for the Gospel of Christ, they laid *everything* down—they left home, family, comforts, education, *and* the hope of getting married.

And even those who did get married were willing to lay down

their husbands and children daily for the sake of the Gospel of Christ. Vibia Perpetua—an early Roman martyr—said goodbye to her husband, family, and infant son in order to give her life for the sake of the Lord who died to save her. Sabina Wurmbrand—the wife of a Romanian pastor during the 1945 Communist invasion—challenged her husband to stand up and defend the name of Jesus, even though it meant ten years of imprisonment, torture, poverty, and separation from the man she loved. Elisabeth Elliot—who had waited patiently for years to finally be married to her husband, Jim—allowed him to give his life as a martyr to the Auca Indians for the cause of Christ, and she chose to forgive them and pour out her life for them, even after his death.

This is what Christ meant when He said we must forsake father, mother, family, and houses in order to be His disciple. Even the most precious gifts He gives us must always be relinquished back to Him with a willing and eager heart. Our fulfillment cannot be found in marriage, children, or fairy-tale dreams come true. Until He is our all in all, we aren't truly living the Gospel life.

And until we are content with Him alone, we aren't truly ready for an earthly romance that will stand the test of time. Why? Because it's all too easy to start clinging to a human instead of to Jesus Christ. And when we cling to a human to fulfill the longings of our heart, we quickly become discontent. Even the most Christlike man cannot meet every need and longing of our heart. And if we expect him to, it only leads to disillusionment. Countless women drive their marriages into the ground by nagging, criticism, and selfish demands because they do not find contentment in the perfection of Christ, but expect perfection from their spouse instead.

Contrary to what most of us believe, our discontentment with singleness can't be solved by finding a guy and getting a ring on our finger. Sure, there may be a short-term high that comes from having someone by our side. But if Jesus Christ is not our all in all, the romance will lose its luster, the temporary fulfillment will fade, and the discontentment will return with even greater force.

Marriage is not the answer to the longings of our feminine heart—Jesus Christ is.

If someone had spoken those words to me as a single young woman, I would have nodded my head in hearty agreement. But like most other Christian single young women today, my life didn't demonstrate that reality. The moment a guy like Kyle came onto the scene, I quickly lost the "Jesus is enough" attitude and replaced it with "Jesus is enough as long as I have a boyfriend and the potential of getting married soon."

So now it was time to make a choice. The soft whisper of Christ's Spirit was convicting me of leaving my first love. He was challenging me to lay everything on the altar before Him, to give up all that I clung to outside of Him, like Mary of Bethany pouring out her precious ointment upon His feet (John 12:1-3).

It was time to not only let go of Kyle—but also of the hope of ever having an earthly romance. It's not that God was telling me I was called to be single for the rest of my life, but He wanted to make me *completely willing* to be single if He so chose—and not just willing, but *eager and delighted* to sacrifice my all for the One who gave everything for me. It wasn't enough to just say, "Sure, Lord, I'm willing to be single if that's what You call me to." I'd said those words for years—but they were just words. It was exactly as Christ said, "These people draw near to Me with their mouth and honor Me with their lips, but their heart is far from Me" (Matthew 15:8). He didn't just want me to say it—He wanted me to live it.

I wrestled with the decision for days.

Here I was, in a perfectly healthy Christian relationship, with a perfectly nice Christian guy. I wasn't technically doing anything wrong or unspiritual. In fact, my romance with Kyle was far more "pure" than most others I'd had in the past. Even our physical relationship didn't seem to be evoking much compromise. Why would I walk away from something so harmless? Why would I voluntarily give up the ability to have a boyfriend, especially a morally upright guy like Kyle, when this kind of guy was so hard to come by?

I realized that the only times I'd ever been single without a guy in my life were the times I'd had no choice. I'd never deliberately decided *not* to have a guy at my side. In fact, whenever I didn't have a boyfriend, I spent most of my time and energy trying to find one.

I knew that to truly allow Jesus Christ to become my all in all, specific obedience was required. I knew what He was asking of me: To end my relationship with Kyle. To not enter another relationship until God made it very clear that it was the one He wanted me to spend my life with. To stop spending my time and energy chasing after guys, daydreaming about guys, or wondering what guys thought of me. And to no longer be on the lookout for available Christian men.

The gentle voice of Christ's Spirit was challenging me to become so completely consumed in my relationship with Him that I no longer pined after an earthly romance. To become so perfectly content in Him that guys were no longer the focus of my existence. To be so fulfilled in Him that I had no urgent need to have someone at my side. To embrace singleness joyfully, no longer seeing it as a curse, but as an amazing opportunity to build my entire life around my heavenly Prince.

I knew there weren't many people in my life who would support or understand this kind of choice. Well-meaning friends and family members wanted me to find a godly guy, get married, and raise children. They weren't trying to pressure me; they just wanted me to be happy. They didn't want me to miss out on all the pleasures of marriage and family. But their concern only left me feeling inadequate and incomplete as long as I remained unattached. I knew their subtle pressure upon me would only increase if I chose to walk the narrow path Christ was calling me to.

Most of the Christian girls my own age were so caught up in the dating scene that they would think of me as mentally unstable if I chose to walk away from it. And I knew there weren't many Christian guys who were interested in a girl with "unusually high standards"; a girl who didn't flirt, date around, or make herself available to every guy who looked her way.

But I also knew that no sacrifice was too great for the Prince of my heart. Just as Paul considered everything that was gain to him as rubbish for the surpassing greatness of knowing Christ Jesus as his Lord (Philippians 3:8), so I was being called to lay aside anything and everything that stood in the way of building my life completely around Him.

There would be plenty of Christian voices in my life that would shout with indignation that such a sacrifice was completely unnecessary and extreme. But they did the same to Mary when she poured out her valuable perfume upon Jesus. Mary did not have the understanding or approval of others, but she had the smile of her King. And I knew beyond a shadow of a doubt which one I would rather have.

The night I broke up with Kyle was one of the most significant nights of my life. I experienced a small taste of what Christ meant when He said, "If anyone desires to come after Me, let him deny himself, and take up his cross, and follow Me" (Matthew 16:24). I'd heard those words all my life as a Christian, but I'd never actually realized that they meant something specific and practical for my day-to-day existence. I was finally seeing things more clearly: Taking up my cross meant deliberately choosing to give up "rights" that other people enjoyed and laying down my own plans, dreams, and agenda in order to make Jesus Christ my first love—not just in theory, but in real life.

As I hung up the phone after telling Kyle I needed to end our relationship, I felt a strange mixture of pain and hope. Ending the relationship had been painful, but not in the same gut-wrenching, heartbreaking, hopeless-feeling way that all my other breakups had been. Rather, it was more like the healthy, positive pain of training for an athletic sport. It wasn't comfortable, but deep inside I felt a clear sense that something amazing was going to come of it. It was the pain caused by obedience to my King, "who for the joy that was set before Him endured the cross" (Hebrews 12:2). For the first time in my life, I was following His pattern. I was willing to gladly endure the pain of self-sacrifice, knowing that unspeakable joy lies on the other side of obedience.

Elisabeth Elliot wrote, "None of us likes pain. All of us wish at times we did not need to 'go through all this stuff.' Let us settle it once and for all: we cannot know Christ and the power of His resurrection without the fellowship of His suffering."[1]

I knew that ending my relationship with Kyle was only the beginning. My King was calling me to walk a path of radical obedience and sacrifice for Him—at least one that *seemed* radical compared to most of the other Christians I knew. This sacred call required me to die daily to my own wants, ambitions, whims, and desires. No longer could I be led by merely my feelings and emotions. Rather, I must be led by the longing to glorify my Lord, no matter what the cost.

That night I not only laid down my relationship with Kyle, but also my obsession with finding a guy and getting married. It's not that the desire to get married magically disappeared the moment I made that commitment, but by the grace of God I was no longer discontent with being single, pining for the day when I would finally meet the right guy and live happily ever after with him. Rather, I began to build my life around my first and most important love story—a daily romance with Jesus Christ.

It wasn't easy to retrain my daily habit patterns. Instead of continually pondering how I could make myself physically attractive to win the approval of guys, I had to train myself to care far more about becoming attractive on the *inside* by the transforming beauty of Jesus Christ. Instead of spending my free time on the phone, at the mall, or on my computer, I had to learn how to spend my free time cultivating my relationship with my true Prince—journaling, worshipping, praying, studying His Word, and reading stories of great Christians. Instead of strategically placing myself in the path of available guys, I had to reprogram my attitude to one that trusted

God to write my love story in His own perfect time and way, without manipulation on my part.

But the amazing thing about all of these painful-yet-rewarding decisions is that I did not have to "become strong enough" to live them out on my own. I found that as I leaned upon the strong arm of my Bridegroom and trusted in His power, He enabled me to live according to His pattern and gave me strength to make difficult choices I never would have been able to make on my own.

Giving up the temporary pleasures of the dating scene and the relentless pursuit of finding the right guy didn't make my life colorless and miserable. In fact, I had never felt so vibrant, joyful, or alive. Jesus Christ really became my all in all—and I found that He was more than enough to satisfy the longings and desires of my heart.

Yes, I still desired to get married and raise a family someday. But those desires no longer controlled or consumed me the way they had before. I was no longer enslaved to my fairy-tale dreams and ideals. I was able to entrust the desires of my heart into the hands of my faithful King and, for the first time in my life, to *leave* them there instead of immediately taking them back out of impatience.

It wasn't easy. There were many lonely nights, wondering if I had made the right choice, wondering if a life of such extreme consecration to Christ was really necessary. But in those moments I would call out to the One who faced the most intense loneliness of all time. He would gently remind me of the struggle He faced in the Garden of Gethsemane. He also had asked His Father if there was any other way—but there was not. And so willingly, joyfully, He had endured the greatest test of all time...all because of His love for me.

That season of surrender was the foundation of everything I have now, from my love story with Eric to my daily intimate walk with Jesus Christ to my message for today's young women. When I laid everything down at the feet of my King, that's when I discovered the beauty and romance of the Christ-life. The moment I died to self's agenda was the moment I truly began to live for the first time.

Obedience, when it flows out of genuine love for Jesus Christ, is never wasted and never regretted. As Corrie ten Boom said:

> Self is a tight lock. I see many decent sinners who are in spiritual prison because their self is on the throne of their hearts, and Jesus is on the cross. What liberation comes when Jesus cleanses their hearts with His blood and comes to the throne, and self goes on the cross![2]

The Pattern of True Christianity
Applying the Gospel to Singleness and Marriage

But all through life I see a Cross
Where sons of God yield up their breath
There is no gain except by loss
There is no life except by death
And no full vision but by Faith
Nor glory but by bearing shame
Nor Justice but by taking blame
And that Eternal Passion says,
"Be emptied of glory and right and name."

AMY CARMICHAEL

There are some who would have Christ cheap. They would have
Him without the Cross. But the price will not come down.

SAMUEL RUTHERFORD

The idea that everything—including the *good* dreams and hopes God has given us—must be surrendered back to Jesus Christ is often deemed extreme and unnecessary. You don't have to look very far these days to realize that this is not a popular message in modern American Christianity. The concept of trusting God to script our love story in His own perfect time, without manipulation on our part, is typically treated as ridiculous and naive. And shooing away perfectly decent guys like Kyle in order to wait for a man completely abandoned to God is viewed by many as a recipe for lifelong disappointment.

A slew of books have hit the Christian market in the last few years that tell young women it's healthy for them to be unhappy and discontent with singleness. These messages say single young women should forsake the misguided idea of "waiting on God" and instead take matters into their own hands to find a husband. (We'll talk about some of these books in greater detail later on.) Their ideas are promoted under a banner of seeming spirituality. These modern voices contend that because God obviously created marriage, and that marriage is clearly a *good* thing in Scripture, that we should not accept an extended season of singleness. They tell us we should view singleness as a curse of our society, not a purpose-filled opportunity from our loving Father.

But what is the pattern of the Gospel?

Christ said, "If anyone comes to Me and does not hate his father and mother, wife and children, brothers and sisters, yes, and his own life also, he cannot be My disciple" (Luke 14:26).

Paul said, "Yet indeed I also count all things loss for the excellence of the knowledge of Christ Jesus my Lord, for whom I have suffered the loss of all things, and count them as rubbish, that I may gain Christ" (Philippians 3:8).

Psalm 73 says, "Whom have I in heaven but You? And there is none upon earth that I desire besides You" (Psalm 73:25).

Once upon a time, Christian men and women understood what it meant to lay down everything for the sake of Christ—including their desires for marriage and family. Like Abraham surrendering Issac, they willingly laid their most sacred and priceless blessings upon the altar before God. They realized that if He desired them to be married, He would make it clear in His own perfect time and way. But He must always come first, and He must always be implicitly trusted.

Jim and Elisabeth Elliot's love story beautifully illustrated this pattern. Their powerful romance is captured in Elisabeth's book *Passion and Purity*. On a chilly winter day in 1947, a young college girl named Elisabeth sat in the school auditorium listening to a passionate speaker. The speaker exhorted his audience not to stir up or awaken love until God initiated the relationship. Elisabeth's heart was pricked by the challenging words. Many of her college friends had already found serious relationships. Some were engaged or married. Elisabeth felt called to a life of service for God, but she couldn't seem to ignore the longing in her heart for an earthly love story.

God was asking Elisabeth to surrender that desire to Him; to give Him the pen of her life and allow Him to script her story...even if it meant a life of singleness. Could she trust Him that much?

"God was sifting me," Elisabeth wrote later. "[He was asking] 'do you want to be worthy of Me? Do you want to know Jesus Christ as Lord?' What kind of a God is it who asks everything of us? The same God who did not spare His own Son, but gave Him up for us all. He gives all. He asks all."

Elisabeth gave her all to Him. She surrendered her longing for marriage. She wanted to be loved, but she also wanted something deeper. The something deeper she wanted was a Christ-ruled, Christ-centered existence. And He was asking for total control. "Lord," she prayed, "here's my heart."

Living out her commitment became even more challenging when she met a fiery young Christian named Jim Elliot. The more she got to know Jim, the more she saw that he was the picture of everything she hoped for in a husband. He was strong, friendly, and handsome, but the supreme dynamic of his life was that he loved God. Nothing else mattered much by comparison.

Soon Jim began to show an interest in her. But God continued to challenge her to surrender the friendship back to Him—not to cling to the hope of a relationship, to leave the pen in His hands. Elisabeth struggled deeply with the challenge. "A settled commitment to the Lord Christ and a longed-for commitment to Jim Elliot seemed to be in conflict," she wrote. "I was only a college girl, trying to do well in my studies, praying for direction for my life, attracted to a very appealing man whose primary interest was in the Kingdom of God. [What was] wrong with that?"

But God wanted everything, even the "good" desires of her heart.

One day Jim told Elisabeth that he was in love with her. The revelation was bittersweet. Elisabeth's heart soared at Jim's words but became sober again when he went on to say that God had challenged him to embrace a life of singleness—perhaps for life, or perhaps only for a season.

Jim told her that he had given all his feelings for her to God, saying that if God wanted them to be married, He would have to make it clear in His own timing. But in the meantime, Jim needed to live as if Elisabeth was not yet his. He spoke of the story of Abraham's offering up of the most precious thing in his life: his son Isaac. "So I put you on the altar," he told her.

Elisabeth and Jim agreed to pray steadily about their future and wait patiently until God made the way plain. Waiting was excruciatingly difficult. Was God interested in the plight of two college kids? Had their cause escaped His notice? Would He really take an interest in this love story when He was busy with so many other, grander things?

Elisabeth and Jim believed God wanted to be involved in the intimate details of their lives and decisions, so they continued to trust. They continued to wait. No matter how strong their feelings were, they would not rush ahead of God.

"A good and perfect gift, these natural desires," wrote Elisabeth later. "But so much more the necessary that they be restrained, controlled, even crucified, that they might be reborn in power and purity for God. For us, this was the way we had to walk, and we walked it. Jim seeing it his duty to protect me, I seeing it mine to wait quietly, not to attempt to woo or entice."

Elisabeth and Jim didn't just wait on God for a week. They didn't just wait a month. They didn't wait for a year. *Five years passed* while the two young people sought God's direction. They remained committed to each other, but they were careful to guard their emotions and pursue nothing more than a Christ-centered friendship until

God showed them otherwise. The road was narrow and lonely. But Elisabeth and Jim understood the difference between self-focused human love and a love scripted by the God of creation.

Elisabeth believed that a man's love for a woman ought to hold her to the highest standard, and that her love for him ought to do the same. She did not want to turn Jim aside from the call of God, to distract his energies or in any way to stand between him and surrender. This was what she understood real love to mean.

"Purity comes at a high price," she wrote. "Sometimes the sacrifice makes little sense to others, but when offered to Him it is always accepted."

Finally, after years of hoping, trusting, waiting, and leaving the pen in God's faithful hands, the Author of romance scripted a new chapter in their love story. He made their future clear. They felt His gentle hand guiding them to serve Him together to reach the unsaved people of South America. They were married in a simple ceremony in Ecuador in 1953.

Was the sacrifice worth it? For all their waiting and radical decisions, did Elisabeth and Jim receive anything better in the end?

Both said an unequivocal yes, praising God for the beauty, the goodness of what He had done between them. Their joy was unspeakable. Elisabeth and Jim's love became a spectacular display of God's faithfulness and sovereignty. The decisions they made in their relationship prepared them for the amazing adventure God called them to in their life together. They had learned sacrifice, self-giving, and implicit trust in their Creator. And soon these qualities would be put to an even greater test.

On January 8, 1956, Jim Elliot and six other missionaries were killed by Auca Indians—men whom Jim had diligently prayed for and sought to serve for six years. He willingly gave his life for the sake of Christ, and his example infused millions with passion for the Gospel.

Elisabeth willingly surrendered her husband to Christ, just as she had done as a college girl in the auditorium that day. His faithful hand had scripted her story, and she knew that even in the midst of intense pain and heartache, His purpose was for her highest good.

After Jim's death, Elisabeth chose to give her life in service to the very people who had killed her husband, exemplifying the principle that she and Jim had built their marriage and life upon: "He is no fool who gives what he cannot keep to gain what he cannot lose."[1]

Jim and Elisabeth Elliot were not the only great Christian couple that walked this triumphant, narrow way.

Oswald Chambers met Biddy, his wife-to-be, during his preparation for the mission field. They shared an incredible kindred spirit and like-minded passion for God, and marriage seemed to be an obvious fit. And yet Oswald knew that his desires must first be fully surrendered to his Lord. Christ must come first, even if it meant they never married. He wrote to Biddy:

> He has all the circumstances in His hand—in His hand my whole life (and yours with me) must be for Him and not for domestic bliss.[2]

Later God *did* direct Oswald and Biddy to marry and labor together in His kingdom, and they had the beautiful satisfaction of knowing that He'd been given His rightful place as Lord over their decision.

Reese and Elizabeth Howells, who led one of the most dramatic revivals in Africa and had a powerful lifelong ministry of prayer and evangelism, felt drawn together by God yet willingly laid their hope of marriage on the altar before Him:

> The Lord had drawn them together, until they wondered if it were God's will for them to marry and make a home for the tramps. Soon after, however, they were led in the opposite direction—to give up their marriage, not knowing whether it would ever be restored to them. [It wasn't until] three years later that the Lord's word came that their lives should be united in His service.[3]

As I mentioned earlier, there are many great Christians, such as Amy Carmichael, Gladys Aylward, and John Hyde, who laid down the possibility of marriage before God, never to have it restored to them. And they willingly and gladly embraced a life of undistracted service to Christ's kingdom.

No matter how our selfish, fleshly side feels about it, laying everything on the altar before our King, and allowing Him to do with our lives whatever He sees fit, is where true Christianity begins.

Our desire for marriage must be no exception. Let us not fall for ear-tickling, lackadaisical messages that require less than absolute abandonment to the One who gave His very life for us. He took up His cross, and He asks us to do the same.

Never forget...on the other side of surrender, we will find the greatest joy!

No Strings Attached

Not long ago I was a guest on a radio program in which I shared about surrendering my love life to God and eventually experiencing a God-written love story. The next day I received an email from a disgruntled listener who wrote, "I am a 39-year-old virgin who has lived my life by God's standards and am still single. I was never one of those people who had a certain career they wanted when they grew up. All I ever wanted to be was a wife and a mom. I am neither. Surrendering this area to God and living in purity has not made my dreams come true—it has only brought me hurt."

Sadly, her story isn't uncommon. It's easy to think, "If I surrender this desire to Christ, He will eventually give it back to me. If I stay pure, then surely He will write a beautiful earthly love story for me and all my dreams will come true."

But that's not real surrender. When I laid down my dreams and desires at the feet of Jesus, I knew I could not hold on to any expectations. I didn't have the assurance that one day He would write a beautiful love story for me. I couldn't assume that an earthly prince was waiting in the wings for me.

Rather, I was to *expect* to be single—and to become fully content with singleness—unless at some point God made it clear that He had a different plan for me.

When I chose to live in purity "all the days of my life," I wasn't making a bargain with God: "I'll stay pure, and in return I want You to write me a beautiful love story." Rather, I chose a life of purity because I wanted to love and honor the Prince of my heart, Jesus Christ—even if He never blessed me with an earthly love story.

When I walked through this process of surrender, God exposed and uprooted every seed of selfishness within my heart. Prior to this season of my life, I had always approached Christ wondering what *I* could get out of my relationship with Him. Now, He was asking me to lay everything down upon the altar, not expecting *anything* in return.

One of the most powerful sermons I ever heard closed with these challenging words, "Why should we come to Jesus Christ? Not for our own benefit. We should honor and serve and love and give our lives to Jesus Christ even if we were to go to hell at the end of the road...*because He is worthy!*"[4]

It's amazing how even the act of surrender can become all about *us*. The woman who wrote me that email is hurt, disappointed, and confused because she made a bargain with God—"If I surrender this to You and live in purity, then I expect You to eventually write a beautiful love story for me." And since it hasn't happened yet, she feels God has let her down.

Christ loved us without expecting us to love Him in return. As He was dying on the cross, those He had come to save were mocking and spitting in His face. Can we love Him the way He loved us? Can we surrender everything to Him without expecting anything in return?

I have discovered throughout my life that our Lord cares very deeply about the dreams and desires of our heart, and He takes great joy in meeting them in His own perfect time and way. Surrendering to Him is not drudgery, but delight. As we abide in Him,

He changes and shapes the desires of our heart to match with His desires for us, as it says in Psalm 37:4.

Following His pattern doesn't leave us with a second-rate version of life on this earth, but a far more glorious, beautiful, and fulfilled one. And yet, even though having the specific desires of our heart fulfilled is very often a by-product of surrender to Christ, it cannot be our reason for pouring out our all upon His precious feet. Our reason must be passionate love for Him, with no strings attached.

Putting Emotions in Their Place

Hannah Hurnard wrote:

> Love is not a feeling. It is an overmastering passion—to cast ourselves down like a waterfall, in happy giving, asking for nothing in return except for the joy of so doing. When we really begin to learn and practice that lesson we shall begin to feel "at home" in the eternal world of selfless love. It is not some special feeling one waits for, nor some special person to evoke the love. It is an attitude of will. I will cast myself down in giving. The lower I go, the more love I am able to transmit from God to others, just like the Lord of love himself, who was not content until He found and took the lowest place in the universe.[5]

As American Christian women, we hear lots of messages today about the importance of our *heart*—messages that put great emphasis upon our feelings, our needs, our uniqueness, and our desires. We are often led to believe it's okay for us to build everything around our emotions and our wants. "Your heart is *good*," is the message of one popular Christian book. "By living out your desires and dreams, you bring glory to your Creator."

But is our heart really good? Should our own feelings, dreams, desires, and emotions be nurtured and coddled the way American Christianity prescribes? I believe our emotions and desires certainly can be instruments of God to help direct our lives, but *only when they are fully yielded to Him*.

Most of us never truly die to self—we never really walk through the painful process of laying every hope, dream, and wish of our heart upon the altar before our King, or of letting our identity become swallowed up in Him. And as a result, our emotions, personality, and desires quickly take over and control us, hollering and bellowing and clamoring for us to build our life around them. So we start dating guys like Kyle because we are following our heart's desire for companionship. We start flirting with available men because we are controlled by the emotional need for earthly romance. We begin dressing seductively because of our inward longing to be found beautiful by a guy. And we forsake a life of total abandonment and service to Christ for a comfortable life of pleasure because our feelings and desires are telling us it's the only way to be happy.

Emotions *must* become subservient to the Spirit of God—to His will, His agenda, His purpose, and His direction. The vast majority of us have become enslaved to our own feelings rather than bond servants of Jesus Christ. We should never make decisions based upon what we *feel* like doing, but on what our Lord is asking of us. Loving Him is first an act of the will, a choice to put Him first, no matter what our feelings tell us. Once we learn to love Him with our will, our emotions and feelings naturally follow suit, and it becomes our greatest delight to give our lives wholly to Him. As the psalmist said, "I delight to do thy will, O my God!" (Psalm 40:8 KJV).

Elisabeth Elliot said it this way: "The difficulty is to keep a tight reign on our emotions. They may remain, but it is not they who are to rule the action. They have no authority. A life lived in God is not lived on the plane of the feelings, but of the will. In Scripture the heart *is* the will—the man himself, the spring of all action, the ruling power bestowed on him by his Creator, capable of choosing and acting."[6]

This is the secret—whether we are single or married—to finding contentment no matter what our situation. To turn down the volume of our selfish, screaming emotions and attune our ears to our King's gentle whisper. To yield to *His* strength rather than the power of our own desires. To *choose* to love, give, serve, and pour out our lives for Him, asking nothing in return. It's what He did for us. And it's what He asks us to do for Him.

If the thought of laying everything (especially the hope of marriage) on the altar before your King, expecting nothing in return, makes you feel apprehensive, depressed, or hopeless, you can be sure those emotions are *not* coming from God. The enemy of our soul is always busy at work, trying to speak words of doom to our minds, whispering that following God's ways will only lead to heartache, disappointment, and disillusionment. He often causes us to believe we are surrendering to a scowling Master who takes pleasure in making us unhappy.

I used to imagine telling God I was willing to be single and then spending the rest of my days in a long, drab gray dress, sitting by the window in a rocking chair, rocking my life away in misery. Or when I imagined giving up my life to serve the least around the world, I used to picture spending my days in a dismal hut in Africa, covered with bugs and lice, wasting away in misery. But those fears merely exposed the fact that I didn't truly know the nature of my God, and, therefore, I didn't truly trust Him with all my heart.

Get alone with your King, meditate upon who He really is, and allow Him to give you His heart and His vision for the beauty of true surrender. It's not a doorway into misery; it's a doorway to abundant life, joy, peace, and supernatural strength. Remember the words of Paul: "He who did not spare His own Son, but delivered Him up for us all, how shall He not...also freely give us all things?" (Romans 8:32). And the words of James: "Every good gift and every perfect gift is from above, and comes down from the Father of lights, with whom there is no variation or shadow of turning" (James 1:17).

My life has never been flooded with so much beauty, adventure, and romance as when I have been fully yielded to Jesus Christ. Remember who He is. His plans for you are good. He wants to give you a future and a hope (Jeremiah 29:11). *But first He must have your will.* And once He does, you will be able to declare with David the psalmist: "In thy presence is fulness of joy; at thy right hand there are pleasures for evermore" (Psalm 16:11 KJV).

[God said to Abraham], "Take now your son, your only son Isaac,
whom you love, and go to the land of Moriah, and offer him there as
a burnt offering on one of the mountains of which I shall tell you."
GENESIS 22:2

There comes a crisis, a moment when every human soul
which enters the Kingdom of God has to make its choice;
when it has to renounce every desire of self, of personal
ambition and worldly benefits—it has to give up all that, and
embrace God, His righteousness and His Kingdom.
CATHERINE BOOTH

I believe that a moment of destiny comes in the life of every child of
God—the moment when God's purpose for your life hangs delicately
in the balance. Death to all that you are...is the only gateway
through which you may enter into the fullness of all that Christ is.
IAN THOMAS

Am I Enough?
Kelly's Story
(age 24)

Have you ever been asked that dreadful question at family parties, work gatherings, or among church circles? You know the question that makes every muscle in your body tense up? The question that makes you look for the nearest exit out of the building? This question has caused more agony in my life than I would care to admit. In the world it is posed as, "So, are you dating anyone?"

The Christian circles put a little spin on the question. It usually comes in the form, "So, has God brought that special person into your life yet?"

Just last week I was asked this very question. I was leading a group discussion on what it means to be set apart for Jesus Christ. I was passionately sharing God's heartbeat for refugees, orphans, and widows. It was a beautiful night with these women as the Spirit of God began opening eyes to His heartbeat for the least of these.

As the evening drew to a close, a middle-aged woman approached me looking very concerned.

Oh, no! What did I say that was offensive? I wondered. It certainly wouldn't be the first time!

"Honey, this was wonderful tonight, but I need to ask if I can pray with you." With that she grabbed my hands.

I was immediately filled with gratitude, as I desired to enter into the throne room of God pleading on behalf of His needy and afflicted. But she had something different in mind.

"You don't have a boyfriend, do you, honey?" she asked point-edly.

"Uh, excuse me?" I replied, wondering what my relationship status had to do with advancing the kingdom of God.

"Let's pray and ask God to send you your husband soon. I know he is out there waiting for you."

In her mind, I was only capable of doing partial work for the kingdom of God because I was without a husband. She hinted that I should be focusing more attention on settling down and getting married.

This is exactly the mind-set that has been instilled and enforced among both secular and Christian circles. We are often told that we are only half usable until we find our other half. So of course we must wait and prepare to meet Mr. Right. In fact, we must spend (or, dare I say, waste) years waiting for him to show up.

I had fallen victim to this mind-set for many years. I stated things such as, "If I had a husband, then I would go overseas on missions." Or, "I would be so much more content if I had a man to share life with."

Really?

It's funny because as God has challenged me to step out in faith as a single woman serving Him, I have realized that this is one of the best seasons in life in which to be doing so. I have one Man in my life whom I serve, Jesus Christ. I have one purpose I can focus on unhindered, which is to see the kingdom of God come down today.

I am free to pack up and go to Cambodia on three-weeks notice. I am free to begin a nonprofit organization helping local refugees. I am free to spend hours undistracted at the feet of Christ. I am free to be single minded.

As a result I have learned that contentment is not correlated with any other relationship besides my relationship with Jesus Christ. I am most content when I see the fruits of the kingdom of God around me, when I see justice, and when I see His salvation come down upon those I love.

After the woman finished praying, she asked, "How hard is it to be in the waiting phase?"

"What am I waiting for?" I asked, though I knew where she was going.

"Well, you know, waiting for God to bring your husband. Do you wrestle with discontentment?"

I smiled, amused at this lady's concern.

I closed my eyes as I began to imagine the day in which I would see my Groom face to face. And then I said, "Well, we are all in a waiting phase for our future husband. He is sitting at the right hand of God, waiting to come back for His bride. I long for His return and the chance to see Him face-to-face. I long to feel His embrace and throw crowns at His feet! I eagerly wait for that day. For now, I will most gladly prepare myself as His bride. And I will joyfully serve Him in the meantime!"

Now, if this conversation happened two years ago I would have answered quite differently. I probably would have become all teary eyed and exclaimed, "I am so discontent waiting! I worry about it all the time! Let's fast and pray until God sends me a husband!"

However, two years ago my life radically changed. The Lord asked me one day, "Kelly, am I enough for you?" Though I wanted to say yes, my discontent heart knew that would be a lie. The truth of the matter was that Jesus Christ was not enough for me. He was not filling my every longing and desire.

Instead of seeking His presence during this time I sought after a man's. Surprisingly, as I entered into the relationship with someone I thought was the man of my dreams, I realized I was still not content. There was something deep inside that was still not satisfied.

It was then that I was challenged immensely with the verse, "In thy presence is fullness of joy; at thy right hand there are pleasures for evermore" (Psalm 16:11 KJV).

The Lord softly prodded my heart with this question, "Do you believe that verse is true? If not, test Me to see if it is true."

I spent the next months of my life seeking what the Lord's presence actually looks like in day-to-day life. I wanted Psalm 16:11 to be true. I wanted to actually taste and see, as David wrote, that the Lord is good (Psalm 34:8). I wanted the intimacy with the Lord Jesus that Solomon wrote about. I wanted to experience the reality of the mystery of the Gospel, which is Christ in me.

I quickly realized that the Lord's presence was not always found in the comfortable places I was used to. Instead, His presence dwelt among the "least of these" that I had grown up ignoring. I realized that in order to gain the presence of Christ, I would have to die completely to myself. I would need to replace my mind with His. I would need to exchange my definition of being a Christian with His. I would have to lay down my dreams for His.

The last two years have been a roller coaster of a ride. Yet I have never been more content as when I am in the presence of the least of these. I have never experienced the depths of joy as I have when I have seen my friends come to know Christ. I have entered into a spiritual realm of living that is truly divine.

As much as I still long for a husband one day, I can for the first time say that it is not what I pursue or even wait for. The longing has changed as well. Before I would long for a man to fulfill my needs, but now my Jesus has done that above and beyond what I could ever dream of. Instead, I long for a husband who can advance the glorious Gospel with me, a husband who will ultimately point me back to a deeper relationship with my Lord Jesus. If there is not such a man, then I am much more content alone.

Two years ago I would wrestle in the middle of the night with anxious thoughts about singleness. But now, it is not the thought of being single for the rest of my life that keeps me up at night. No, it is the thought that there are still almost three billion people without the Gospel of the Lord Jesus. It is the fact that there are local refugees who are victims of abuse and who still need to be healed by my Savior. This is what consumes my thoughts and my life. And it's a much more fulfilling passion to have than wondering when I'm finally going to meet my man!

My Sister's Wedding Day
Melody's Story
(age 32)

I t was my sister's wedding day. I had dreamed with her about this moment for so many years. I had walked with her through her journey to find true love and prayed and cried with her each step of the way. Now, the day we'd both been waiting for had finally come. It was a perfect day. She was radiantly beautiful, and every detail of her love story had been faithfully scripted by God. With happy tears I helped her into her wedding dress and smiled up to God with thanks for answered prayer. Yet, even as I did so...the enemy attacked, and unwanted thoughts leaped into my mind.

"Why are you standing here helping your *younger* sister with her wedding dress, while you are still single," the voice of self-pity began to badger me. "I bet God has completely forgotten you when it comes to love."

Years ago I'd surrendered this area of my life to God. I had joyfully embraced a life of singleness for as long as He desired it for me. And He had been more than faithful to me each step of the journey. Now, the voice of my "surrendered will" began to take a stand against the tempting voice of self-pity.

"God has not forgotten me!" I shot back with conviction. "Not only do I think He can do this for me in His own perfect time...I am sure He can do even better than anything I have yet dreamed!"

"But look, Mel, you're older than your sister!" Self-pity's voice was relentless. "And you aren't getting younger. Don't you think it's a bit too late now?" Old fears I had thought were crucified and nailed to the cross were obviously not so dead after all. But I continued to meditate on the faithfulness of my God and stood my ground.

"I may be getting older, and he is too, if he's out there! But that only means I'm that much closer to an amazing miracle if God so wills. With God, nothing is ever too late!"

"Well," self-pity's voice continued with a heavy sigh, "I just hope you're prepared. It may be a few years...in fact, it may not ever happen at all."

I breathed a quick prayer, and then I almost laughed to myself as I gained new strength.

"A few years.... a hundred years! I don't care! I only want a love story if it's God's will anyway. And besides, I'm much too happy to sit around and feel sorry for myself. So let's not even go there."

Self-pity slipped away in defeat, and I smiled to myself in peace. There was *no way* I was going to let those unwanted thoughts mess up my life, let alone this beautiful day. My younger sister's wedding day became one of the happiest days of my life.

I'm 32 years old—well past the age I thought I would still be single. I've continued to grow through experiences of both joy and pain, and I still haven't met my Prince Charming. But my life is so full and complete in Christ—I couldn't be happier. I've been privileged to travel to many different countries around the world doing health work and evangelism. I've watched hundreds of Kenyans go under the water in baptism simply because I chose to step out of my comfort zone and go to the bush in Africa to speak the simple Gospel words written on a projector screen. Here in the United States, while by profession I am a nurse, my real profession is ministry. I've prayed with hundreds of my patients and have watched some give their life to Christ. There is no greater joy! Many people tell me enviously that I'm so lucky I'm single and can do all these things. Some of these people married right out of high school, some have married more than once, and some have marriages that they have found to be less than fulfilling. Of course, even for them there is still hope for more; yet I have to say it's true...I'm not "lucky" but "blessed" because I've allowed God to do with my love life what He saw best.

A few years ago there was a guy in my life whom I was very like minded with, and he was aimed toward the mission field just like me. I'd grown up with him, and I had actually prayed for more than eight years that, if it was God's will, He would bring us together. However, my hopes and dreams for earthly love came crashing down when he, who also had never dated, started dating one of my close friends. They were later married, and they asked me to be in their wedding. By God's grace, I could stand in full support...even though my own world had shattered. (We are all still very close friends to this day.) But God had a purpose for this heartbreak experience... and it was through this, the death of my vision, the death of my way, that He really became even more real in my life.

Suddenly, with overwhelming clarity, I realized how God felt about me—how much He loved me and longed for me to truly be in love with Him. And instead of dreaming of the marriage vows I hoped to someday share with an earthly prince, the passion of my life began to focus more and more around the vows I should be saying and living daily with my heavenly Prince.

While it hasn't all been easy, I know God gave me this season of singleness for a purpose—to not only help me grow up, but also to grow my character in Him. I realize now that the purpose of my life was not just to "have a romantic marriage" or even to "have a partner in service." (Both worthwhile ambitions.) But the purpose of my life that God has patiently been seeking to show me over the years was to find my fulfillment in Him—to be fully surrendered and yielded to Him, His plan, and His purposes. It's kind of funny, but sometimes I wonder if I still even want to get married. Imagine that? Sometimes I think...if I got married would I still keep the same sweet fulfilling relationship with Christ I have now? Would a husband encourage me in this walk, or would he be jealous? Of course, I know if God wills for me to marry, the "right man" will be seeking that for me too. In the meantime, if I never marry, it's okay. I have found my true love, and I couldn't ask for more.

My encouragement to my single sisters…

Don't let the world distract you. Everyone says, "Why aren't you married? Why aren't you dating?" I'd tell them why, and then they would tell me, "Your standards are just too high. You are too picky!" Sometimes I believed them. I tried a little of the "Internet getting acquainted scene." Yikes! I felt as though I were in the midst of a school of sharks and, of course, everyone was only putting their best foot forward. You didn't see them in everyday life, and once I did (with one guy that I met online), I realized how incompatible we really were. Good matches have resulted from such sites, but I encourage all the single girls I know to stay away from "Internet dating." God knows our hearts, He knows our needs, and He can bring that person into our life at the right place and the right time, even if we are in some remote village in a Third World country. So my philosophy is, if God hasn't brought that person along, it's not the right time. Keep focusing on growing in Him, and don't worry about what others say or about all the "lovebirds" around you.

Our society is sick, and it tends to try to cripple those healthy singles still around, saying you aren't complete alone, or you have to have a partner to be happy. But it's a lie. Even if you get married, you aren't going to find your complete fulfillment and happiness in your partner. And if you try to, you'll be disappointed. No one could ever make me happy the way God does.

So we need to get out of this mind-set that we are only "half whole" and realize that we are complete in Christ. And even if you're scared of the dark (like me), with God by your side you can go to the jungle all alone and face the scary unknown for the sake of Christ. It's incredible!

Also, life is not all about having the best body, trying to stay young, and trying to impress the world. It's about living completely and only for your King. Of course, the devil tries in a thousand ways to distract us from this goal with friends, careers, security, fear, fashion, possessions, entertainment, and even natural dreams of building a home and nest, but if it keeps us from the Bible and from time on our knees, we are doomed to a life of discontented singleness. If we can break past these obstacles, the sky is the limit for possibilities!

Finding Romantic Fulfillment
Discovering the Ultimate Bridegroom

O LORD, You are the portion of my inheritance and my cup.
PSALM 16:5

Jehovah is my shepherd, I do not lack.
PSALM 23:1 YOUNG'S

For He satisfies the longing soul.
PSALM 107:9

A spirit of restlessness and resistance can never wait, but one
who believes he is loved with an everlasting love, and knows that
underneath are the everlasting arms, will find strength and peace.
ELIZABETH ELLIOT

Tiffany is a 28-year-old single woman who gave her life to Christ as a child. One of her greatest desires has always been to get married and raise a family, and growing up she always expected to marry young. She is a lovely brunette, and she has not had a shortage of men interested in her over the years. But the right one has not yet come along. As much as she desires an earthly love story, Tiffany has not put life on hold until she meets her future husband. Rather, she has devoted her single years to Jesus Christ, giving her time and energy to serve the poor, the lonely, and the outcast around the world. Tiffany deeply desires to be married—but she is not bitter or discontent toward her situation. She is radiant, joyful, and full of life. She has an inner glow that exudes the love of Jesus Christ. She emanates confidence and fulfillment. She has found what most young women today are desperately seeking—and she has obtained it without having a guy in her life.

Rachel is a young woman in a very similar situation as Tiffany—but with a very different outcome. Rachel gave her life to Christ at a young age and always expected Him to write a beautiful love story for her in her late teens or early twenties. But now she is nearing 30, and nothing has happened yet. And the disappointment and impatience have taken their toll. Rachel is an attractive girl, but she exudes a sense of unhappiness and insecurity that diminish her physical beauty. She rarely smiles. She has spent her twenties floundering about from one living situation to the next, never really feeling comfortable or settled about what she should do with her life. When Rachel talks about God, you can hear sarcasm and bitterness in her tone. Sure, she's still a "Christian" and she still goes to church, but it's obvious she and God aren't on intimate terms. Rachel is very similar to the 39-year-old woman who wrote to me after the radio interview—she feels God has let her down, and she's letting the whole world know it.

Two single young women—two very different stories. What makes the difference between Tiffany's radiant version of singleness and Rachel's embittered one? Plain and simple...*a love story with Jesus Christ.*

In my book *Authentic Beauty,* I wrote about the time in my life when I finally discovered the fulfillment of all my romantic childhood hopes and longings; when I finally found the prince I had always dreamed of to carry me away to his castle and cherish me forever. Since many of my readers knew about my love story with Eric, they at first assumed that when I spoke of my prince, I was talking about him. But as I explained in *Authentic Beauty:*

> My true Prince is not Eric. My true Prince is Jesus Christ. Eric, with all his amazing qualities, could never meet the

deepest needs inside my heart the way my true Prince has. If not for the tender love of my true Prince, my love story with Eric would not have even been possible. The romance of my love story with Eric is only a faded glimmer of the spectacular beauty of the love story I share with my Jesus Christ. In fact, my childhood longing to be loved and cherished by a tender knight that I could follow to the ends of the earth was placed in my heart by Him. Jesus Christ alone can fulfill that desperate longing.[1]

Jesus Christ was not merely a stand-in until Eric came along. Jesus was, and still is, my true Prince, my ultimate Bridegroom, and my all in all. Yes, Eric does bring wonderful joy and fulfillment into my life, but my love story with him could never compare to my love story with the King of all kings. Jesus Christ is the One who ultimately satisfies the deepest needs and desires of my heart. Jesus Christ is the One I lean upon for fulfillment, strength, and security.

I have no guarantee that Eric will always be around—God may call him home before me. And though he is an amazing husband, there will always be moments when he fails, when he falls short of being the sensitive, devoted, picture-perfect prince of my childhood fairy tales. But Jesus Christ is the same yesterday, today, and forever (Hebrews 13:8). He knows my heart better than even I do—because He created me. He will never fail me. He will never disappoint me. And He will always be the most perfect Prince my feminine heart could ever crave.

When I speak about this concept to single young women, sometimes I hear the response, "Well, that's easy for you to say. You're married. It's much harder to make Jesus Christ your first love when you struggle with loneliness every single day."

But recently I heard a twentysomething single woman say the exact opposite. "I'm so thankful that God hasn't brought my husband along yet," she told me. "It's *because* I've been on my own that

I've really learned to really make Jesus Christ my first love, my all in all. Now I know how to lean upon Jesus Christ for everything—comfort, strength, security, peace, and joy. And I know that's the best foundation I could ever have for marriage—total dependence upon Jesus Christ for everything and not on another human."

If only more single young women would catch a vision for this amazing season of life, just as this woman did! As Paul said, "There is a difference between a wife and a virgin. The unmarried woman cares about the things of the Lord, that she may be holy both in body and in spirit. But she who is married cares about the things of the world—how she may please her husband" (1 Corinthians 7:34).

Singleness is an incredible opportunity to be fully consecrated in body and spirit to Jesus Christ alone—to be undistracted by any other romance and free to be consumed with Him. And, as mentioned earlier, this is not only an amazing opportunity for our single years, but it is the absolute best way we could ever prepare for marriage. When Jesus Christ is our all in all, we will never place unhealthy pressure upon our spouse to meet the needs only He can fill. And if our husband is ever taken from us, we will not lose our confidence, hope, or security because it's in Jesus Christ.

In my book *Set-Apart Femininity,* I wrote about Sabina Wurmbrand, whose husband Richard was imprisoned and tortured for ten years because of his stand for Jesus Christ. For ten years this amazing woman did not know if her husband was alive. She was imprisoned herself for four years, and then she was left on the streets without any way to buy, sell, or get employment. Her life was unspeakably difficult, and her marriage certainly wasn't something out of a storybook. Though her husband dearly loved her, she could not lean on him for daily strength and comfort. He couldn't buy her roses or even express his love to her during those years of torture and confinement. And yet she remained just as joyful, radiant, fulfilled, and outward focused once Richard was taken away from her as when he was by her side. Why? Because Jesus Christ was everything to her.

Sabina's heavenly romance with Christ far outweighed her earthly romance with Richard. Her daily intimacy with the Prince of her heart carried her through the most dark and lonely nights. She didn't just survive those difficult years—she triumphed through them. Her life was a glorious display of supernatural love and power to all those who encountered her. She led thousands into the kingdom of God—all because she was willing to lay down her every hope, dream, and expectation for earthly romance and allow Jesus Christ to be her all in all.

Corrie ten Boom tells of a conversation she had with a struggling single Christian woman.

"There are some, like me, who are called to live a single life," Corrie told her. "God blesses them with absolute contentment. Others, like my friend Ellen, are called to prepare for marriage which may come later in life. They, too, are blessed, for God is using the in-between years to teach them that marriage is not the answer to unhappiness. Happiness is found only in a balanced relationship with the Lord Jesus."

"But it is so hard," the woman said, her eyes filling with tears.

"That is so," Corrie replied. "The cross is always difficult. But you are dead, and your life is hid with Christ in God (Colossians 3:3). Dear girl, it cannot be safer. That part of you which would cling to a husband is dead. Now you can move into a life where you can be happy with or without a husband—secure in Jesus alone."[2]

Putting Jesus Christ first is not something that comes easier when you are married. Whether we have a man in our life or not, it is *always* a challenge to silence the selfish demands of our whims and emotions and become consumed with Him alone. But until we do, we aren't truly ready for an earthly romance. And often God will hold off bringing our future husband into our life until our heart is fully His.

In previous books I've written about the dangers of idolatry. Idols are not just bronzed statues that people bow to in ornate temples. An idol is anything that claims our heart, focus, and attention above

Jesus Christ. And for the majority of women, the biggest temptation toward idolatry is our longing for earthly romance. (Note: Some modern messages for single young women downplay the idea that marriage dreams can become idols in our lives—we'll talk more about this later.)

Whether it's the fairy-tale dreams we've held on to since childhood, a specific guy we have our eye on, or even the man we pledged our life to at the altar—earthly love can all too quickly become the central focus of our lives. That's why we so easily get our hearts broken and our dreams shattered—because they are wrapped up in the wrong love story. Earthly romance becomes an idol that consumes our heart, emotions, time, and focus. All the while the most perfect love story with the most heroic Prince of all time is right there waiting for us.

The Secret to Beautiful Love Stories

When William and Catherine Booth (the founders of the Salvation Army) became engaged, a close Christian friend spoke these words about their romance:

> It is one of the most remarkable and charming love stories in the world—the love story of a man and a woman in whose hearts an extraordinary sense of Christ had the uppermost place. To this couple, everything secular and human is secondary, for God and His worship is the sovereign focus of their existence.[3]

If you want a remarkable human love story, *fall in love with Jesus Christ*. Being passionately in love with Jesus Christ is the only thing that makes an earthly romance truly beautiful. But most of us have it backward—first seeking to fulfill our heart's desires with a human love story and then attempting to add on an intimate romance with Jesus Christ. Unfortunately, it doesn't work that way. Jesus is jealous for first place in our lives—and He must not be placed behind anyone or anything, including our husband. That is why He said that in order to follow Him, we must forsake our families, houses, and all that we have.

Colossians 1:18 reminds us of the position He must have, in every single area of our lives: "In *all* things He may have the pre-eminence" (emphasis added). Preeminence literally means "to hold first place." I challenge you to ask yourself this one question today: Does Jesus have first place, or is it the hope of an earthly romance that you hold most dear to your heart?

Madame Jeanne Guyon wrote:

> Abandonment is practiced by continually losing your own will in the will of God; by plunging your will into the depths of His will, there to be lost forever! Abandonment must reach a point where you stand in complete indifference to yourself. The attitude will bring you to the most wonderful point imaginable—where your will breaks free of you completely and becomes free to be joined to the will of God! You will desire only what He desires.[4]

As I've interacted with countless girls in my generation, I have found that single young women usually fall into one of two categories: Those who are joyfully abandoned to Jesus Christ, and those still clinging to their own agenda. Tiffany's version of singleness versus Rachel's version. Young women like Tiffany, who have a thriving love story with Jesus, are joyful, happy, radiant, and fulfilled. It doesn't mean they never experience loneliness or the longing for a human love story. But with every pang of loneliness and every wistful longing for marriage, they lean all the more upon Jesus Christ and find that He is ready and willing to satisfy the cry of their heart—day or night. As the Song of Solomon beautifully portrays:

> Who is this coming up from the wilderness, *leaning* upon her beloved? (Song of Solomon 8:5, emphasis added).

If you are longing for romantic fulfillment in your life, look no further than Jesus Christ. There is no other way to find what you are searching for, even if the most gorgeous and gallant man carried you away to the most glorious castle in the world. If you never get married on this earth, you can be the most romantically satisfied woman in the world—when Jesus is your Bridegroom, the Lover of your soul. And if you do get married on this earth, your love story can be a beautiful reflection of the greatest romance of all time. Either way—*a love story with Jesus Christ is the key to romantic fulfillment.*

A Love Story with Jesus
Giovanna's Story
(age 28)

There were years when I didn't want anything else but being married. I was angry all the time because it seemed there was no chance it could happen. I always felt lonely. I had to go to bed alone; I had to wake up alone. I didn't have anyone who could hug me or kiss me in the way a husband would. I mean, I had my entire family and my church and my friends—but I still felt insecure, and I thought the only way I could stop feeling like that was to be married.

But one day, like a Gentleman, so tender and so delicate, Jesus showed me that everything I was looking for and everything that was missing in my life and in my heart was not going to be fulfilled by some guy. He showed me that even if I met someone and got married, I was still going to feel empty and insecure. I had known Jesus since I was little, but I had never experienced Him in that close, intimate way.

But He was there all the time! By my side! He was taking care of me! He had made all the beautiful flowers for me. He wanted to have a relationship with me, and He used everything to make me fall in love with Him: the moon, the rain, the mountains. The Creator of the Universe was trying to catch my attention, and I was looking for something else!

Thank God for all of His grace to deliver me from my own foolishness! Now I am absolutely madly in love with Jesus. I'm sooooo in love with my Savior, and now I know He is the only one who will never fail me, He is the only one who will always be there to listen to me, to laugh with me, to cry with me, to hold me, to hug me, to help me...

I used to make fun of people who sang alone in their cars. Now, I sing all the way whenever I go. I know that even when it appears that no one is with me, the One I'm singing to is *always* there to hear my love songs for Him.

Part Two

The Dangers
of Modern Voices
The Gift of Singleness Redefined

The Modern Church and Singleness

A Breeding Ground for Discontentment

Those who look to Him are radiant, and
their faces shall never be ashamed.
Psalm 34:5 ESV

Kaylie is a frustrated 24-year-old single who recently told me, "Our church just announced that they are starting a singles' 'support' group. They make it sound like singleness is some kind of 'problem' that needs to be fixed! I'm really tired of hearing that attitude everywhere I go."

Angela, a 26-year-old single, shares Kaylie's frustration. "People seem to always hint that I'm incomplete or inadequate because I'm not married yet. Christians treat me as inferior, even if they don't mean to. The church is geared for married couples with kids. Singles' groups seem to mainly exist for the purpose of helping you get paired up with someone so you won't be single anymore."

The "Problem" of Singleness

It's a bleak irony that countless Christian single women face. They struggle daily with surrendering their dreams for marriage back to God and being content with singleness. They come to church hoping to find love, support, and encouragement, but often the very people who should be cheering them on in their life of abandonment to Christ are the ones who overlook or disregard them because they are not married yet. I've heard many single young women say that being around Christians only seems to breed discontentment, impatience, and insecurity, rather than joy, inspiration, and strength for the journey.

There is no question that modern Christians are insensitive to single young men and women. American Christianity does not encourage or support the concept of letting God orchestrate your love story—especially once you are older than 25. At every turn single girls are invited to Christian singles' groups where they can meet available men, told about online Christian dating services where they can be matched with their soul mate, or given books about how to become more "dateable" so they can find their perfect prince.

Our Christian culture breeds discontentment with singleness.

As I said earlier, the message of absolute surrender and finding fulfillment in Christ is not a popular one in our modern American Christianity, especially when it comes to singleness. There is endless pressure—both from outside and inside the church—upon single young women to take matters into their own hands when it comes to marriage. It comes in a spiritual-sounding package. "God created marriage. He is the one who gave you the desire to be married. So why don't you just do whatever you possibly can to help the process along and find a husband? After all, it's what God created you for. He *wants* you to go out there and meet guys, date around, and join online dating services. When you search for a man, you're doing what He created you to do!"

These messages resonate with our fleshly, selfish nature—the part of us that craves to be in control of our own lives and satisfy the desire of our heart outside of God. And if we can justify this "take it into my own hands" attitude under the banner of it being God's design for us, that makes it even more appealing. Young women who choose to "embrace their season of singleness" or "wait on God for their spouse" are deemed ignorant and naive. They are subject to mockery and criticism from people in the church.

Why?

Well, the sad reality is that American Christianity is in crisis.

Once upon a time, Christianity was made up of men and women who turned the world upside down for the kingdom of God and lived in total abandonment to Him. They actually believed He took interest in their daily lives, and they trusted Him to meet their every need. They were ready to give up everything at a moment's notice to bring glory to their King, and their lives were full of power, life, and victory.

But that's not the reality we live in today.

Most of us have inherited a faith that has no real life or power. Instead of zeal there is apathy. Instead of courage there is timidity. And instead of confidence in God there is paralyzing doubt. You can't just walk into any evangelical church these days and expect to hear undiluted truth. Rather, it's far more likely that you'll hear a sappy, watered-down, twisted redefinition of Christianity that tickles the ears but leaves the soul dead. The Gospel is being redefined nowadays to imply that God is okay with our self-focused, sin-addicted, pleasure-seeking lives. The Bible is no longer deemed the authoritative Word of God, but a humanly scripted narrative that can be edited and changed to mean whatever we want it to mean.

All of this has had a great impact upon the modern church's approach toward singleness.

Many young women assume that if a book has been published by a Christian publisher, and is being sold in a Christian bookstore, that its message has already been carefully scrutinized by a task force of elders and pastors who are committed to protecting the integrity of God's truth. Having been intimately involved in the Christian book industry for the past 14 years, I can tell you unequivocally that this is simply not the case. Just because a book is written by a Christian author and is being sold in a Christian bookstore does not mean that it is filled with God-honoring, timeless biblical truths. I have found that the large majority of modern Christian books are dripping with human psychology and human ideas, but are devoid of the true Gospel of Jesus Christ. Historical, biblical, power-filled, world-changing Christianity is becoming extinct among modern voices.

I have seen all too many Christian young women base their mentalities and decisions about singleness and marriage around faulty messages they have heard from modern Christian writers and leaders with devastating results. How we choose to approach this area is perhaps the most important decision we'll ever make in our life apart from choosing to follow Christ. So it is absolutely vital that we listen only to voices that honor God's pattern and have the true Gospel foundation at their core. When it comes to books and teachings on singleness, there are a lot of lies floating around out there under the banner of solid Christian wisdom. In this section of the book, I would like take a closer look at these dangerous errors and compare how they stack up against God's truth.

As I said earlier, a handful of Christian books on singleness have hit the market in the last few years that have attempted to speak to our secular culture's growing disregard for the importance and sanctity of marriage. These books highlight some important truths: They speak against the indifference toward marriage prevalent in pop culture and encourage us that marriage was designed by God and should be held in high esteem. They emphasize the importance of God's command that we "be fruitful and multiply" through marriage and family, rather than merely pursuing a career and cultivating the independence our culture pushes. They rightly declare that our desire for marriage is not wrong but healthy and God given. And they remind us that God designed *marriage* (not premarital flings or platonic friendships) to meet our desire for love, partnership, sexual intimacy, and companionship.

These books also speak to the issue of modern masculinity, empathizing with the countless young women who are surrounded by self-focused men who don't seem to value marriage or even pursue it anymore, and proclaiming that this is not a reality we should accept.

I wholeheartedly agree!

But these well-meaning writers have misidentified the culprit behind the diminishment of marriage in today's world. They admit that our sinful, godless society is partially responsible for the modern decline of marriage sanctity—but they don't stop there. They also point an accusing finger at the church's classic teaching on biblical, God-centered singleness.

And therein lies the danger.

These writers contend that if we are among those who actually believe God has a purpose and plan for our singleness, we are guilty of diminishing the importance and sanctity of marriage. Some even go as far as to say that if we choose to joyfully embrace our singleness as a gift from God, we have been duped by Satan himself.

Principles such as waiting on God's perfect timing for marriage, trusting in Him to orchestrate the details of our love story, and finding contentment and purpose in singleness are not only being questioned by these authors, but also openly mocked.

Here's a quote from one book that challenges single women to "rethink the gift of singleness":

> The belief that remaining single is legitimate and godly is a work of the devil. Read that again: Satan dishonors marriage by fooling us into believing that singleness is okay.[1]

The author commends Calvin's view of singleness:

> [Men] and women who are not connected in marriage are like the mutilated members of a mangled body.[2]

Wow. Talk about putting pressure on young women to shed the stigma of singleness! They've actually been fooled by Satan if they think that their singleness is legitimate and okay! Their singleness is far more than just a stigma—it has actually made them like the mutilated members of a mangled body! If that's the case, they'd better hurry up and find a husband at all costs, so they can finally be in God's perfect will and get out of such a horrible pit!

And, sadly, all too many single young women settle for a mediocre guy like Kyle or for someone even worse because of messages like this one. As my husband, Eric, says, "If a young woman follows that kind of advice, she's more than likely going to end up with a total jerk for a husband!"

That book isn't the only Christian voice out there sending these kind of confusing signals to today's young women.

In another book that explains what single women can do "to help marriage happen," the author explains her message like this:

> This is not just another book about seeking fulfillment in your singleness. As beings created in God's image, we were designed for relationship—that's why extended singleness leaves so many women discontent. It's also why we should be intentional about finding fulfillment in marriage...many singles over-spiritualize their single state, thinking it's more holy to look to God alone for fulfillment. But that's inconsistent with how He made us.[3]

The message is simple: Christ is not enough to provide the fulfillment we long for. If we try to find contentment in our singleness, we are merely over-spiritualizing something God never intended. Unless we have been specifically called by God to the lifelong path of celibacy that Paul chose, we will never be truly satisfied until we find our spouse.

Do you see anything amiss with this idea?

Now, if these kinds of books were only being read by women who had embraced the arrogantly-independent, look-out-for-number-one, exalt-career-over-marriage-and-family kind of attitude, their messages would hit the mark a lot better. While I still don't think their approach to the subject is completely biblical or healthy, I do agree that awakening "independently minded" women to God's sacred intent for marriage is tantamount.

But the problem is that the hyper-independent, career-above-all-else woman is not the only kind of woman reading these books. In fact, I believe that type of woman, at least in Christian circles, is by far in the minority. After traveling this country extensively for the past 14 years and working closely with multiple-thousands of young women, I have not found that the church today is overflowing with single women who have sworn off marriage in exchange for selfish pursuits. Rather, the church is overflowing with young women who are wallowing in discontentment, putting their lives on hold until they finally meet their spouse, and assuming that marriage is when their "real life" will begin. And when that kind of young woman reads a Christian book that says she should be discontented with her singleness and actively pursue finding a husband, the results can be disastrous.

Just this past week I had a conversation with a Christian counselor who said, "I see so many single young women in my office who are completely missing out on God's amazing purpose for this season of their lives. Because they are completely preoccupied with finding a husband, they don't see how they can be happy until they find one."

For the majority of young women today, Satan has not "duped them into accepting their singleness." (In fact, the single young women *I've* encountered who have accepted their singleness as a gift from God are radiant, joyful, and fruitfully changing this world for His kingdom!) Rather, Satan has duped single young women into believing they can't really live or be happy until they are finally married.

We can never evaluate the correctness of a message based on how it makes us feel. Messages about getting rid of our singleness and rushing out to find a husband might "feel good" to our fleshly, selfish, impatient side, but they do not line up with the pattern of the Gospel. And if we heed these messages, they will only bring heartache to our lives in the end.

Because so many confusing things are being taught today about singleness, I would like to address the errors head on. In the next few chapters, we'll take a closer look at some of the common errors that have pervaded modern Christian messages and stack them up against the pattern of the Gospel.

Contentment in Christ
Is it Really Possible?

As the deer pants for the water brooks,
So pants my soul for You, O God.
PSALM 42:1

A Chinese pastor was thrown into solitary confinement for more than a year because of his faith. Day after day, week after week, month after month he crouched in a tiny cell hardly big enough to stand up in. He remained there in total darkness. There was no light, no human companionship, and no human conversation. It was just him and God.

When he was finally released, he had nearly gone blind from the long lack of light. His body was weak and fragile. But his face was radiant and glowing. He seemed to effervesce with joy and peace. His Christian friends peppered him with questions. "How did you survive solitary confinement for so long? What was it like?"

The frail pastor paused and then smiled. "It was like a honeymoon with Jesus!"

What an incredible statement! Here was a man who had gone more than a year without any kind of human contact—and he'd never known such peace and fulfillment! He was more than satisfied by the sweet fellowship with the Lover of his soul.

He understood that Jesus truly was all he needed. Jesus became, in reality, his all in all. And he didn't just survive those difficult months—he triumphed through them!

If it's possible for a man like this to be perfectly satisfied with

Christ only, then it is certainly possible for you and me! Yes, it's true that God designed us for relationship with others. It's true that for most of us, He designed us for marriage. But it is *not* true that He alone isn't enough to fulfill us at the deepest level, even if *every* form of human companionship is stripped away.

The Error—He Is Not Enough

One of the lies floating around today, whether it comes in the form of a modern teaching or simply the whisperings of the enemy, goes something like this: *Jesus Christ is not enough to fulfill the longings of your heart. When you look to Him alone for satisfaction and contentment, you are fighting against the way God made you and merely trying to "over-spiritualize your singleness."*

One of the books I quoted from earlier says it this way:

> [We've all heard] marriage won't meet all your needs, marriage won't fill the emptiness, you can only find fulfillment in God. Each one of these statements is true. But they are missing something; they're missing the context of Adam's problem. If it's true that God is all we need for fulfillment, then no one was in a better position to be fully satisfied than Adam...He was in a prime position to find all the answers, to fill all the emptiness, and to have his needs met in unbroken relationship with the Creator of the universe. Still, God looked down and saw something out of sync.[1]

Discovering the One Who Fills All in All

No matter how intelligent or spiritual the error sounds, here is the reality of God's Word...Jesus is enough! He is our all in all—whether we're married or single! The fact that God created marriage, and that we are to esteem it as a holy institution, is evident throughout Scripture. Yes, it was not good for Adam to be alone, but was that because God Himself was not enough to fulfill Adam's needs? Certainly not! As the Bible explains, God created Eve because Adam needed a *helper*, a companion to do the work on earth God had called him to do. Yes, there were many blessings and benefits that came to both Adam and Eve through their companionship with each other, but their marriage was never to take the place of God. He was still God, and He was still meant to be their first and primary object of love and worship.

- Psalm 73:25 says, *Whom have I in heaven but You? And there is none upon earth that I desire besides You.*
- Psalm 16:11 says, *In Your presence is fullness of joy; at Your right hand are pleasures forevermore.*
- Psalm 107:9 says, *He satisfies the longing soul.*

David the psalmist had plenty of female companionship in his life. But it is David's intimate relationship with *God* that brings him the perfect satisfaction these verses portray.

Throughout the Bible Jesus Christ is shown as the perfect fulfillment of our heart; the sweetest satisfaction for the human soul. He is called the One who fills us all in all; not the One who fills us halfway so our spouse can fill us the rest of the way.

Marriage was not designed to make up for what God lacked. It was not that God was unable to meet the longings of Adam's heart, so He had to create Eve. Rather, He created marriage to be a *reflection* of the perfect union and fellowship that we have with Him. The entire Bible is a love story—a romance between Jesus Christ and His bride. God is a God of romance. Our earthly marriages are meant to showcase the ultimate marriage that we will one day share with Him—just as the Song of Solomon so beautifully portrays. But even if we never experience earthly marriage, we can be completely fulfilled by an intimate romance with our Beloved Prince, Jesus Christ, the Lover of our soul. He and He alone is the One who fills *all in all*.

In my book *Set-Apart Femininity*, I gave a list of all the things the Bible says Jesus is to be to us. Here is a recap:

My Portion, My Maker, My Husband (Isaiah 54:5), My Well-beloved (Song of Solomon 1:13), My Savior (2 Peter

3:18), My Hope (1 Timothy 1:1), My Brother (Mark 3:35), My Helper (Hebrews 13:6), My Physician (Jeremiah 8:22), My Healer (Luke 9:11), My Refiner (Malachi 3:3), My Purifier (Malachi 3:3), My Lord, Master (John 13:13), My Servant (Luke 12:37), My Example (John 13:15), My Teacher (John 3:2), My Shepherd (Psalm 23:1), My Keeper (John 17:12), My Feeder (Ezekiel 34:23), My Leader (Isaiah 40:11), My Restorer (Psalm 23:3), My Resting Place (Jeremiah 50:6), My Meat (John 6:55), My Drink (John 6:55), My Passover (1 Corinthians 5:7), My Peace (Ephesians 2:14), My Wisdom (1 Corinthians 1:30), My Righteousness (1 Corinthians 1:30), My Sanctification (1 Corinthians 1:30), My Redemption (1 Corinthians 1:30), My All in All (Colossians 3:11)[2]

Wow. Talk about the ultimate Bridegroom! Such a Prince is more perfect than any fairy-tale hero that ever existed. And He invites us to have a daily romance with Him! He delights to become all of those things to us on a daily basis! And if we are in such intimate fellowship with our Lord that He fills us all in all and becomes everything in that list above, then we certainly will not try to satisfy the longings of our heart some other way!

Let me point out here that the vast majority of us *are* called to be married. In saying that Christ wants to be our all in all and that we are not to look to marriage to meet needs only He can fill, I'm certainly not trying to downplay the sacredness or significance of getting married. But, as mentioned earlier, the principle of finding our fulfillment first and foremost in Christ is crucial, even for those of us who are called to be married one day.

Here's why.

The Bible makes it clear that married women are to be helpers to their husbands—to honor them, respect them, serve them, and help meet their needs. Unfortunately, most married women are so busy trying to somehow make their husband into the picture-perfect man of their childhood fairy tales that they don't spend much time thinking about how they can selflessly love and serve their man.

Just as single women can all too easily try to solve their deepest longings by finding a man, married women can fall into the same trap—nagging and manipulating their husband in an effort to change him into their fairy-tale ideal. But a woman who is fully satisfied in Christ is free to selflessly love and serve her husband with unconditional love. And this kind of woman will have far more ability to help shape her husband into a Christlike prince than a nagging, self-focused, emotionally needy wife ever could.

Don't fall prey to the lie that Jesus Christ is not enough to fulfill the longings of your heart. The most satisfying, spectacular divine romance with Jesus awaits us if we simply allow Him to be *everything* to us. This powerful statement from Charles Spurgeon says it beautifully. (I changed the masculine pronouns to the feminine in this quote to make it even more personal for you.)

> The [set apart young woman] not only acknowledges Jesus to be her King, but her heart is full of loving devotion to Him as such. Nothing can make her heart leap like the mention of that august, that more than royal name. She remembers what Jesus did, how He loved her, and gave Himself for her; she looks to the Cross and remembers the streams of blood whereby she was redeemed, even when she was an enemy of God. She remembers Christ in heaven, enthroned at the right hand of the Father, and she loves Him there, and it ravishes her heart to think that God hath highly exalted the once-despised and rejected One, and given Him a name that is above every name, that at the name of Jesus every knee shall bow, of things in heaven, and things in earth, and things under the earth. She pants for the time when the Crucified shall come in His glory, and rule the nations as their liege Lord. She loves Jesus so that she feels she belongs to Him altogether, bought with His blood, redeemed by His power, and comforted by His presence; she delights to know that she is not her own, for she is bought with a price.... She loves her King, and loves

Him with an ardor unquenchable, for many waters cannot drown his love, neither can the floods quench it.[3]

Today I Am

Rather than being preoccupied with solving the dilemma of our singleness, God's Word says we should be consumed with loving, knowing, serving, and worshipping Jesus Christ. It may sound impossible to become excited and fulfilled in your singleness, but I guarantee that if you submit your mind, will, emotions, and desires to Christ, He will supernaturally enable you with the joy and peace you need in order to walk this narrow road.

My amazing sister-in-law, Krissy, lived out her single years one day at a time. When her brother Mark asked her once if she was called to singleness, her response was, "Today I am." She didn't worry about the next ten years; she trusted God for the grace to live joyfully and contentedly for that day alone, knowing she would have everything she needed.

I've encountered many radiant single young women who are completely unconcerned with the disapproval and opinions of others. They don't get ruffled by the singles' support groups all around them. They aren't shaken by the subtle pressure of friends and family members to hurry up and find a guy. Why? Because they understand that their bodies are living sacrifices to the King of all kings. They have become the bond servants of Christ. They are ravished and captivated by their soul's Husband.

Young women fervently in love with Jesus Christ aren't worried what other people think—their eyes are seeking only the applause of heaven. And, like Christ, they approach every circumstance in life with the knowledge that their heavenly Father is handling the situation—their role is not to manipulate or control. Their role is merely to yield themselves fully to Him. And they have found great joy in this abandoned life, so much so that they truly embrace singleness as a gift, rather than resenting it as a stigma.

I'm not talking about an arrogant feministic "I don't need a man in my life" kind of attitude. And I'm not talking about losing all desire for marriage and family. I'm simply talking about a joyful yielding to Jesus Christ, trusting in His perfect timing, and building your life and focus around Him rather than the pursuit of marriage.

Don't take the advice of the modern Christian culture to "hurry up and get married already." Don't be riled by the insensitivity of friends and family. Take the advice of Paul (in 1 Corinthians 7) and discover the incredible opportunity awaiting you in your single-ness—whether for a season or for a lifetime.

And remember that God is enough.

If you need a little extra encouragement for the boundless frontier that singleness can provide, just read the stories of some amazing *single* women who radically transformed this world for the kingdom of God. Some of my favorites are Gladys Aylward, *The Little Woman*; Jackie Pullinger, *Chasing the Dragon*; Elisabeth Elliot, *A Chance to Die: The Life and Legacy of Amy Carmichael*; and Corrie ten Boom, *The Hiding Place* and *Tramp for the Lord*.

My Soul's Husband

Annie's Story
(age 25)

About a year ago, I was out on a walk through a neighborhood filled with families and couples with either their children or dogs in tow. I walked past them and waved with a smile upon my face, but deep down a pang of longing and ache were increasing with each step. The waiting season for my future husband seemed as though it were reaching an unbearable length, and I silently cried out, "Lord, I would give *anything* to have a strong, tender, manly hand cradling mine on this walk. Where is he, Lord?"

From the time I was a little girl old enough to esteem the wonder and beauty of a fairy-tale romance, I have waited in anticipation for my own unfolding love story, my day to walk down the aisle, and pursuit of the greatest marriage of all time. Throughout the intense years of growing up and having every hope of such a pure, beautiful story threatened, I have held unwaveringly in faith that God could and would script such a legendary romance. Yet with the passing of years, it began to dawn on me that marriage wasn't just a natural event that occurred conveniently after graduation or even in my early twenties. There was life to be lived right here and now, either spent pining and waiting for a husband or living a fulfilled life with my Savior each day.

However small a thing it may seem to be, my beloved Jesus' response to me on that walk was priceless. It was an unexpected reply, but more real to me than the couples I had walked past. "Hold

Mine," He whispered. "It's here and always has been waiting to be the strength, care, love, and presence that comforts you, upholds you, rejoices in you, and guides you. Reach out and you'll see I am more real than you have ever known."

At this crossroad, I was either going to keep sighing and sitting in hopes that my prince would soon come along or live out what the Lord was showing me increasingly in His Word. He said He was a very *real* presence? With Him was fullness of joy? There was safety under His own wings of protection? Being with Him is a fountain of life? Everything I needed for life and godliness was found in Him? His love better than life itself?

A smile still comes to my face when I think about how I responded. My eyes closed as tears began to fill them up and a smile that reached clear to my soul graced my once downcast expression. He *was* there to be all that His word promised. My companion, my protector, my comfort, my joy inexpressible, and the strong Bridegroom I had so longed to have at my side. At His heroic invitation to walk with Him hand in hand I gently squeezed my hand closed around His, gripping by faith the nearness of my Groom. It was then that a wonderful and altogether lovely joy filled up my heart as the walk with this very real Prince extended through the sunset.

That day took me deeper into experiencing Christ as my first love. It was the smallest gesture of my grand King, but it might as well have been a walk through palace gardens. Every day since then God gives me the same invitation, to meet Him in reality as I go throughout each day. To rise with Him, start the day with Him, follow His lead with each friendship in my life, share with Him every thought, hear His words of guidance, love, and wisdom, pour out my heart in prayer, lean upon His power to live as He calls me to, and lay down upon my pillow with His strong, protective presence right there with me.

I had spent hours envisioning the life I would have serving alongside an earthly husband. We would be rescuing dying bodies and souls, taking loads of orphans into our family, and while he preached the Gospel I would be praying fervently for the Holy Spirit to move upon lost hearts. And while those dreams still exist, they have taken a new place in my heart. Rather than taking up each moment with waiting, they lie tucked away, joyfully and sacredly kept for the proper time, and when an earthly man is given every single one of those dreams will be possible with our Lord.

What now takes center stage is that my soul's Husband is the very One who has healing for those dying bodies and hope for each perishing soul, the Father to every fatherless child, and the Gospel itself living and active! At His bidding and enablement each day I can be His hands and feet. He's already given me grand adventures following Him to the orphans in Haiti, standing before officials in communist China, and seeing through His eyes a crippled leprous woman. And He has won my heart with His never-failing presence, matchless love, and fulfillment of every promise I have believed Him for!

Dare I say it…I am now so completely captivated by the love of this heavenly Man that I want no earthly man until it will only serve to bring my first love greater glory on this earth! And I know now that my heavenly love story with Jesus Christ will be the greatest gift I can one day give my future husband as we will both simply keep living fully for our King…together.

6

Giving God a Hand

Isaac or Ishmael?

"Not by might nor by power, but by My Spirit," says the Lord of hosts.
ZECHARIAH 4:6

It is better to trust in the LORD
than to put confidence in man.
PSALM 118:8

Give us help from trouble,
for the help of man is useless.
PSALM 60:11

Some trust in chariots, and some in horses;
but we will remember the name of the LORD our God.
PSALM 20:7

Probably the biggest fear that single women deal with is that if they don't take matters into their own hands, they will miss every opportunity to be married. Today's guys are not well trained in the art of winning, pursuing, and cherishing the heart of a woman. And, oftentimes, women feel that they are in a game of "survival of the fittest" in which the available men quickly get claimed by the most aggressive women, while the ones who guard their feminine mystery and focus on Christ alone get passed over.

Modern voices and the urgent whisperings of the enemy don't make this battle any easier. An all-too-common error floating around out there goes something like this: *Because God created the majority of us for marriage, it also stands to reason that we as women are supposed to pursue marriage, to be strategic and intentional about finding a husband, and to "give God a hand" in finding our spouse.*

Take a look at this quote from a modern Christian book on singleness:

> *You'll get married in God's perfect time, so just relax.* Here's that "wait on the Lord" idea again. We must stop thinking that because God knows the end result, we can rely on Him to work out everything in between...we are not just called to sit back as He works out the details. We cannot use good theology as an excuse to get out of the responsibilities we must take to secure our own futures—whether it means finding a job, a house, or a husband.[1]

Or this from another book on helping women get married:

> Getting married isn't something that's "nice if it happens." Marriage is what most of us are called to pursue.[2]

Leaving the Pen in His Hands

Here is the truth that many of us hesitate to really believe: If and when the time comes for us to be married, *God will orchestrate the love story.* But in the meantime, our focus is to be on serving Him and pouring our life out for Him, not on getting serious about getting married. The timing is up to Him, not us.

Why am I so convinced that we are to remain fully dependent upon Christ in every area of our life, including this one? Because Jesus left us an example that we should follow in His steps (1 Peter 2:21). And as part of His example to us, Jesus did nothing of His own volition, but only what the Father told Him to do, and only when the Father told Him to do it:

> Jesus answered and said to them, "Most assuredly, I say to you, the Son can do nothing of Himself, but what He sees

the Father do; for whatever He does, the Son also does in like manner" (John 5:19).

What strange words to come from the King of all kings! He could do nothing of Himself? The One who created heaven and earth? It's not that Jesus was actually helpless—it's that He deliberately chose to be completely dependent upon His Father for every word, every choice, and every action. He said:

> The words that I say to you I do not speak on My own initiative, but the Father abiding in Me does His works (John 14:10 NASB).

As Ian Thomas so eloquently explained:

> The Lord Jesus acted at all times on the assumption that His Father was handling the situation, and Jesus simply took care to obey His Father's instructions. Even when He was being reviled and tortured, "He left His case in the hands of God" (1 Peter 2:23). By this submission to His Father, Jesus "learned obedience" (Hebrews 5:8) as a Man, and the obedience was total; "He humbled Himself and became obedient to the point of death—even the death of the Cross" (Philippians 2:8). Now, as God, He asks the same of you and me.[3]

Certainly it is a great idea to pray for our future spouse and to be obedient to God's voice as He guides our steps in the process of finding a mate. Trusting God to orchestrate our love story doesn't mean shunning men or avoiding friendships with the opposite sex.

But marriage is *not* what we are called to pursue. Sure, it might sound appealing, but it's not what God says. Paul tells us in no uncertain terms what we are called to pursue: "Flee youthful lusts; but *pursue* righteousness, faith, love, peace" (2 Timothy 2:22, emphasis added). Jesus, when counseling the rich young ruler, told him exactly what he should pursue: "Go your way, sell whatever you have and give to the poor, and you will have treasure in heaven; and come, *take up the cross, and follow Me*" (Mark 10:21, emphasis added).

When Paul speaks about single young women, he says, "The unmarried woman cares about the things of the Lord, that she may be holy both in body and in spirit" (1 Corinthians 7:34). He does not say "the unmarried woman is called to pursue marriage," but rather the unmarried woman is called to pursue "the things of the Lord." While Paul is certainly not against women marrying (he even *encourages* younger women to marry in 1 Timothy 5:14), nowhere in Scripture does it say that marriage is what we are called to *pursue*.

It may sound spiritual to use the argument that since God created us for marriage, He has no problem with us being impatient, unhappy, and discontent until we find a husband. It may be easy to believe that He applauds us when we take matters into our own hands and try to help the process along.

But that's not the pattern of Scripture.

When God promised a son to Abraham in his old age, Abraham did what seemed only natural to do—he tried to give God a helping hand. After all, God had said that He wanted to give him a son. What was so wrong with using the good common sense that God had given him and sleeping with his wife's maidservant? It was the only way, as far as Abraham could see, that God's desire for him to be a father would ever happen. The thought of just waiting around until Abraham and Sarah were both on death's doorstep was laughable. As the common saying goes, "God can't steer a parked car!" Abraham bought that very lie hook, line, and sinker. (By the way, God can make bread out of stones and dry land out of an ocean— somehow I don't think steering a parked car is much of an issue for Him.)

So Abraham did what countless single young women do—he tried to help God out, tried to speed things up, tried to use the resources he had to make God's plan happen. And he ended up not with the son that God had promised him, but with his own humanly crafted solution...*Ishmael*. Ishmael was not God's perfect plan for

Abraham's legacy. Rather, God said of Ishmael that "he shall be a wild man; his hand shall be against every man, and every man's hand against him" (Genesis 16:12).

God told Abraham that He would establish his seed through a child named Isaac that would be born to him and his wife Sarah in their old age. Abraham's response was, "Oh, that Ishmael might live before You!" (Genesis 17:18). Like so many of us, Abraham longed for his *own* handiwork to be blessed by God, rather than having to wait for God to fulfill His promise in His own time and way. God challenges us to let Him write our love stories in His own time and way, and our immediate response is, "Oh, that I could just create my own story and have You bless it!" That's what our selfish nature craves. But our Lord has something far better in store, if only we will trust Him.

Allow the Spirit of God to search your heart. Are you trying to create an Ishmael of your own making? Are you attempting to give God a hand in finding a guy and getting married? Do you really believe that Christ can fill you all in all? And are you willing to make Him your first love, even if no earthly love story comes your way?

These are difficult questions to face. But remember that God cares more about this area of your life than even you do. He wants first place in your heart not to make you miserable, but to bless you beyond all you could ask or think. Just read the rest of Abraham's story—when God's promise of Isaac actually came to pass—and be reminded of the loving, faithful, awesome God you serve! A heart centered upon Christ is not a sentence of death—it's a doorway into abundant life, into the most glorious romance you could ever imagine.

When Eric's sister, Krissy, was in her early thirties and still unmarried, she received an endless amount of advice and pressure from well-meaning friends and family members to take matters into her own hands and "find a husband." People gave her the impression that she wouldn't really be happy until she was married, or that she wasn't really following God's pattern unless she settled down with a nice guy. They even counseled her to leave the ministry God had called her to and move to a bigger city, join a singles' group, and make herself more available to men. It was excruciatingly difficult for Krissy, because one of her greatest desires was to be married and have children. And yet she was determined not to manipulate her situation or take the pen out of God's hands. She believed that if it was God's intention for her to marry, He was able to bring her husband into her life out of nowhere, without the help of singles' groups, blind dates, or Internet matchmaking sites.

In the meantime, she refused to put her life on hold or wallow in discontentment and misery because she was single. As a result, her single years were full of radiant life, intimacy with Christ, and eternal impact for the kingdom of God. Because she was willing to trust Him completely, Krissy received the reward of her patience and waiting! She is now married to a wonderful man and has three beautiful kids. What joy Krissy would have missed, both in her single years and in experiencing a truly God-written love story, if she had taken people's advice and ran out to find herself a husband!

How to Find a Christ-Built Man

Christ-built warrior-poet men are not usually found in the singles' scene or on the prowl for women with all the rest of the self-focused, pleasure-seeking guys. Rather, they can be found on their knees in private prayer and worship of their King, fighting for the cause of the least and the outcast around the world, or pouring out their life to build the kingdom of God. And if you give yourself to these very same activities, you are far more likely to meet the man of your dreams than if you put everything on hold until you find a spouse. (We'll talk more about this in the next section.)

Additionally, Christ-built men are not hoping and praying for an aggressive woman who flirts and flaunts, but for a truly set-apart woman who jealously guards her feminine mystique. The "survival of the fittest" game is merely an illusion. The men who are really worth waiting for both understand and appreciate set-apartness. In fact, they are just as eager to meet a Christ-centered woman who is not chasing after guys as you are to meet a Christ-built man who is not chasing after women.

What about when a potential mate comes onto the scene? Should you completely ignore him? Or should you strategically find ways to get on his radar screen?

Most modern Christian advice would attempt to empower you—give you all sorts of practical tips for getting the guy's attention and building a friendship with him and letting him know you are interested. But what is the pattern of Scripture? As I discussed in my book *Answering the Guy Questions*, the entire Bible is a romance between Christ and His bride. And in that romance, He is the initiator—we are the responders.

I've met countless married women who wish their husbands were stronger leaders in their relationship. But oftentimes those same women didn't allow their man to lead at the very beginning of the romance. *They* became the initiators, dropping hints, pursuing a friendship, constantly pushing the relationship to the next level. When we as women become the aggressors, we rob the guy of his God-given position as the leader, and we diminish his masculinity. We will be far happier if we allow him to win our heart, rather than chasing after him and offering ourselves to him without waiting for him to pursue us.

That's not to say that we can never strike up a conversation with a godly guy we'd like to get to know. It doesn't mean we can't be friendly, encouraging, and warm toward him. We don't have to act aloof and disinterested. We just need to let him take the lead.

Here is how Elisabeth Elliot summarized it:

> Wait on God. Keep your mouth shut. Don't expect anything until the [man's] declaration is clear and forthright.[4]

What About Ruth?

Some modern Christians who contend that we should help write our own love story point to the biblical story of Ruth as an example of a woman who pursued a man for marriage, or at least a woman who was clever enough to "help" the process along. One modern author describes the dilemma she faced when she found the man she wanted to marry, but he seemed oblivious to what a good match they were. She turned to a trusted mentor named Mary for advice:

> Prior to listening to Mary, I believed that it was enough to "trust the Lord with all my heart" and "seek first His kingdom." She assured me those things were essential, but she didn't stop there. "Sometimes you have to pull a Ruth," she told me.[5]

The author goes on to describe how she attempted to follow the example of Ruth in drawing the attentions of the young man she had her eye on. She strategically positioned herself to be around him more, invited him to a dinner party, and continually thought of ways he might notice her strengths. It began to work, and soon they were spending quite a bit of time together—as friends. Two months passed, with no official sign from him that he wanted a romantic relationship. Finally, she gave him an ultimatum. One day she flat out told him:

> Steve, I want to get married, and I hope it's to you. But if it's not, then we need to stop spending all this time together. Otherwise, no one else will ask me out—they think we're dating.[6]

The author said that she knew in her heart that she and Steve would make a good match, but that she also knew "palling around wasn't getting me any closer to my desire for, and calling to, marriage."[7]

So she took matters into her own hands. Of course, that's not how she would describe it. She says merely that she "pulled a Ruth." So let's take a closer look at Ruth's example. (If you need a refresher on this story, just read the book of Ruth.)

At first glance, Ruth's approach to Boaz seems fairly proactive, even aggressive. She lays down near him in the middle of the night while he's sleeping—after they've only had one conversation. Talk about being forward toward a guy! But when we take a closer, deeper look at the story of Ruth, we discover that she is anything but a calculating, marriage-seeking woman.

In the beginning of the story, Ruth is a Moabitess who is married to a Jew. When her husband dies, she cleaves to her mother-in-law, Naomi, and refuses to leave her side, even when Naomi decides to return to her own people in Israel. This was not just an emotional attachment to her dead husband's mother. Rather, Ruth recognized that Naomi's God was the only true God. She knew that in order to serve the one true God, she must leave behind everything—her home, her family, her friends, even her very heritage as a Moabitess, and take on an entirely new identity. She says to Naomi:

> Entreat me not to leave you, or to turn back from following after you; for wherever you go, I will go; and wherever you lodge, I will lodge; your people shall be my people, and your God, my God. Where you die, I will die, and there will I be buried. The LORD do so to me, and more also, If anything but death parts you and me (Ruth 1:16-17).

It was a complete emptying of self. An absolute surrender and abandonment to serve Naomi and Naomi's God with every breath from that day forward. A laying down of all her own pursuits, dreams, and identity. And an amazing picture of what God desires in our attitude toward Christ. Ruth was not looking out for her own interests or her own dreams—she was yielded and subservient to Naomi the very same way we are to be yielded and subservient to our King.

Throughout the rest of the story, Ruth is sensitive and obedient to Naomi in the very same way that we are to be sensitive and obedient to the Spirit of God. She does not pursue Boaz because she wants to find herself another husband and he seems like a good catch. Rather, Naomi asks Ruth to become the catalyst of redemption for the family. Ruth could have had her pick of younger, more desirable men, but Boaz was the only kinsman of Naomi who was willing to redeem their family line and rescue them from the poverty and shame that had come upon them.

It wasn't about Ruth's desires—it was about obedience.

Instead of chasing after younger men to fulfill her own needs, Ruth allows her will to be swallowed up in Naomi's.

Ruth's attitude was one of yielding all selfish desires and submitting, not only to Boaz himself, but to Naomi as well. Naomi asks Ruth to lay aside her own desires and become the catalyst for redemption. She willingly submits to Naomi, saying, "All that you say to me I will do" (Ruth 3:5).

Ruth is not self-promoting toward Boaz. Rather, the first time he speaks to her, she *falls on her face and bows down to the ground*, saying:

> Why have I found favor in your eyes, that you should take notice of me, since I am a foreigner? (Ruth 2:10).

Talk about honoring and serving a man's position! Ruth is the opposite of an aggressive, take-the-lead kind of woman. Instead, she is utterly self-effacing and humble—beyond what most of us could ever imagine. Her attitude reflects that of Christ's when He made Himself nothing and took on the form of a servant (Philippians 2:7).

When Ruth uncovers Boaz's feet and lays down as he sleeps (in obedience to Naomi), it's a profound statement, not of forwardness, but of the utmost humility and submission. Listen to this biblical commentary:

> Women of the East, when going to be with their lawful husbands, would, through modesty, and in token of subjection to them, go to the foot of the bed, gently raise the covers, creep up under them to their place. In the case of Ruth, she was merely to uncover the feet of Boaz and lie down there until he should discover her presence and tell her what to do.[8]

When Ruth made herself known to Boaz, it was not to fulfill her own attraction or need for a husband. Rather, it was an act of selflessness and sacrifice. As the commentary continues:

> All Bethlehem knew that Ruth was a virtuous woman, for remaining a widow was one of the greatest proofs of purity to Jews. No doubt many young men, rich and poor, had sought her hand in marriage, but she had refused them. Boaz blessed Ruth...for being willing to take him, an older man, instead of rejecting him for a younger one, rich or poor.[9]

Ruth appealed to Boaz as a kinsman-redeemer for Naomi's family line. It is not that she was saying, "I want to get married, Boaz, and I hope it's to you." Rather, she was saying in essence, "I am willing for you to *purchase* me as your wife, that Naomi's family name might be redeemed. I offer my body as a living sacrifice."

She was giving up her own pursuits and desires and offering to become a bond servant. Just exactly what Christ asks us to do when we take up our cross and follow Him.

That's why Boaz praised Ruth for her virtue, and that's why he marveled that she did not follow after younger men. "May you be blessed of the LORD, my daughter. You have shown your last kindness to be better than the first by not going after young men, whether poor or rich" (Ruth 3:10 NASB). She was pouring out her all on the altar in order to receive him as a kinsman-redeemer. She was sacrificing her own desires and allowing herself to be purchased and redeemed. It's a beautiful and profound picture of our attitude toward Christ—much like Mary of Bethany pouring out her most priceless treasure upon Jesus' feet. Ruth was not a woman who saw a guy she liked and helped the process along until he noticed her and became interested in her. Ruth was a woman who sacrificed *everything* to follow God's will for her life.

And because she laid her all on the altar, she was immensely blessed. Just as we will be, when we lay down our own pursuits and whims and yield completely to God's voice alone.

Can you trust God enough to wait for His direction, His timing, and His best? Can you yield to His design and allow the man He has chosen for you to take the lead, be the pursuer, and be the one to win your heart? Do you believe that God is more than capable of awakening a man's heart toward you when the time is right? Can you wait for your Isaac instead of rushing ahead and creating an Ishmael?

If you aren't willing right now, ask God's Spirit to transform your attitude and make you willing. It's a prayer He delights to answer.

Back to that question of what we should do when it comes to this area of our lives. Ruth provides an amazing example: Yield. Submit. Let go of our own agenda. Don't chase after available men. Humble ourselves. Watch. Pray. Listen. Obey.

And then sit back in wonder as God does His amazing work.

Holding Out for God's Best
Kristina's Story
(age 25)

The church was beautifully decorated. The bride, my good friend Katie, was a picture of loveliness. Outwardly everything seemed perfect. Watching Katie's father escort her down the aisle, I was reminded of the many long talks Katie and I had shared about this very day. We often talked about our future husbands, and our mutual desire to marry men who had a deep love and passion for the Lord. Katie and I clearly saw the need to wait on God's best for our lives, regardless of what others around may do. I remembered the unforgettable day that my dear friend and I had made the commitment to settle for nothing less than God's perfect will in our relationships.

While listening to Katie exchange vows with the man who would soon be her husband, my mind was filled with uncertainty. I wanted to be happy for her, but it was so difficult to ignore the gnawing sense of worry that was flooding my mind. This man who was now placing a ring on Katie's finger was not the husband she dreamed of and prayed for. He did not have the deep love, passion, and devotion for Christ Katie once desired in a mate. She had lowered her standards and was now doing what she committed to never do. She was settling for less than God's best.

Katie has fallen in love with a man who clearly did not have God in first place in his life. She and I talked about this decision, and Katie felt everything would work out all right. She was tired of waiting on the "ideal" mate that she was once committed to. She was now doubtful that such a person even existed.

As the preacher pronounced them husband and wife, my thoughts shifted to my own life. I was approaching my young adult years, and many people were beginning to question when I would be married. The worry I had previously felt for Katie was now replaced with worry about my own future. Not only was I not engaged, but there were no prospects in sight. As I went home from the wedding that day, I told myself that although Katie had not waited on God's best, at least she was married. I began to convince myself that everything really would work out all right, and maybe they would go on to live happily ever after. But deep inside I knew the truth.

That's why it was no surprise when Katie called a few months after the wedding and tearfully confided that she was miserable in her marriage. However, it *was* a surprise that she blamed God for all of her marital problems and refused to take any personal responsibility. Katie was married to a man who had very little interest in church, prayer, or the Word of God. Because these things remained a vital part of Katie's life, she was very unhappy. Her husband was frustrated and angry because of her demands that he be involved in church. But Katie was blaming God, asking why would God allow this to happen to her.

As Katie shared her marital trials, God had my full attention. Everything was not working out all right. The love they had for each other was not enough. God was showing me an up-close example of the tremendous need to wait on His best, even if it means many seasons of singleness. My heart broke for my friend as I thought about what she could have if she had waited for the wonderful love story God had planned for her life. It also saddened me that she refused to acknowledge that it was her own sin, selfishness, and impatience that contributed to her troubles. But, primarily, I was grieved and disappointed in myself for taking my eyes off of Christ, and trying to rationalize Katie's choice.

Since my talk with Katie that afternoon, there has been a pattern of ongoing problems in her marriage. She is now convinced that the promise and commitment to wait on God's best we made as teenagers was nothing more than an unrealistic fantasy. However, I believe that could not be further from the truth. Through Katie's life I have seen the devastating consequences of running ahead of God's will. I have also seen in the lives of others the extraordinary, rich, and rewarding blessings that come when the choice is made to not settle for the standards this world defines, but instead to wait on God's perfect, flawless will.

It has been three years since Katie's wedding day. I am still single, and just as it was then, there are still no prospects in sight. Many still ask the "marriage question." In fact, it seems that as I get older, the questions and expectations increase. However, I am determined that the expectations of others will not alter the commitment that I have made to my heavenly Father. My Father cares so much for me that He took the time to number the hairs on my head. I am confident that God does have a perfect will for my life, including whom and when I will marry. My present focus is learning to fall in love with Jesus, allowing Him to show me areas of my life that are not pleasing to Him, and ridding those things from my life. I am also learning to daily deny self and to pursue an intimate and passionate relationship with God, who has an amazing plan for my life. And for today, that wonderful plan has called me to singleness.

Marriage Above All Else
Exploring the Issue Of Idolatry

Put to death your members which are on the earth: fornication,
uncleanness, passion, evil desire, and covetousness, which is idolatry.
COLOSSIANS 3:5

That in all things He may have the preeminence.
COLOSSIANS 1:18

In my book *Authentic Beauty* I wrote about the danger of pursuing human love over a love story with Jesus Christ. I talked about the principle behind my favorite verse, Psalm 37:4: "Delight yourself in the LORD and He will give you the desires of your heart." This beautiful Scripture illustrates the loving faithfulness of our Lord. As we dwell on Jesus Christ, He fills our heart with *His* desires for our life, and we are completely fulfilled by *Him*.

But most of us have it backward. We aggressively try to meet the desires of our heart by pursuing romantic relationships, popularity, comfort, material possessions, or achievements instead of truly delighting in Jesus Christ.

Even God-given desires can gain an unhealthy hold over our heart and life, like the longing to finally experience a beautiful, God-written love story with one person for a lifetime. As precious as this dream is, it is all too easy to make this desire the focus of our life. As a result, we miss out on experiencing the most beautiful love story of all time with our true Prince, Jesus Christ.

The reality is that the only way to discover the true beauty of a God-written love story with another person on this earth is to delight in Jesus Christ with all our heart, soul, mind, and strength—to find our security and joy in Him alone. Rather than focus all our efforts on the pursuit of a human relationship, we must center our life on the *pursuit of intimacy with Jesus Christ*. As we discussed earlier, only out of intimacy with our heavenly Lover can the beauty of a God-written human love story be experienced.

Marriage Dreams and Idolatry

Some modern voices contend that since the desire for marriage is God given, it can't really become an idol in our lives. The message goes something like this: *The idea that marriage can become an idol in a young woman's life is overblown. When a young woman pines after marriage, she's not making it an idol, she's just doing what God intended her to do!*

One of the books I quoted from earlier says it this way:

> [The notion that marriage dreams can become idols] has been blown out of proportion, and suggesting the possibility of idolatry has done more harm than good. Sadly, the "marriage as idol" warning prevents many young women from gratefully sharing in what God created as good.[1]

The author goes on to give this advice about idolatry:

> How can a Christian woman be sure that her desires for marriage don't drag her into idolatry? For starters, by looking at what the Bible says about it. Almost every one of the more than two hundred idol verses are about objects made of wood, stone, silver or gold...Considering this overwhelming focus on statues, the first and most obvious thing a woman can do to avoid making marriage an idol is never to bow down to one of those plastic bride and groom miniatures that goes on top of a wedding cake.[2]

Let's take a closer look at idolatry from God's perspective.

What Idolatry Really Is

> "[She] went after her lovers; but Me she forgot," says the LORD (Hosea 2:13).

The Bible is perfectly clear: Anything that captures our heart, time, focus, and affection above Jesus Christ is an idol in our life. The desire to get married is not an idol in a young woman's life, but the *obsession* with getting married is.

We are to have no other gods before Him. That doesn't mean we are simply to avoid bowing to a physical object. It means we are to place nothing above Him—not people, possessions, dreams, ambitions, hopes, or anything else—*nothing* should take first place in our heart, mind, and focus other than Him. Marriage dreams *can* become an idol in our life—the thing we look to for fulfillment, hope, and security rather than Christ. And we must be on guard against letting those desires usurp Christ's position in our life.

One of the ways that you can tell something is an "idol" or "other lover" in your life is that you are *unwilling to let it go*; you can't picture living without it.

In all things, He must be first. If our desire for marriage is first and He is second, our desire for marriage has taken a wrongful place in our heart, plain and simple.

G.D. Watson said this:

> When you are so possessed with the Living God that you are, in your secret heart, pleased and delighted over His particular personal, private, jealous guardianship over your life, you will have found the vestibule of heaven.[3]

Dear sister, He is jealous over you! He wants your whole heart. He is the most noble Hero, the most gallant Bridegroom that ever was or ever will be—and He wants *all of you*. Will you begrudge Him this sacred request?

What About God-Given Desires?

Even after choosing to find contentment and fulfillment in your singleness, the desire for marriage does not usually go away. For me, even after I experienced a daily beautiful, satisfying romance with Jesus Christ, I longed for an earthly love story even more intensely than I had before. Once I experienced the intimate fellowship Christ intended me to have with Him, I desired to experience the same kind of intimacy through a Christ-centered earthly love story. Were my desires wrong?

Elisabeth Elliot wrote about laying her desires for marriage to Jim upon the altar before God:

> A good and perfect gift, these natural desires. But so much more the necessary that they be restrained, controlled, even crucified, that they might be reborn in power and purity for God.[4]

That was the very path God called me to as well. Since God created marriage, and placed within us the intrinsic desire for human love and companionship, I realized that the desire to be married, in and of itself, was natural and God given. The key was how I *responded* to my desires. In the past I'd allowed those desires to consume my thoughts and control my actions and decisions. Now I had to learn to thank God for the desires He had placed in my heart and then surrender them back to Him. He showed me that it was entirely possible to long for a human love story and yet not be controlled by that longing.

I observed Krissy closely during her single years. She was an amazing example to me. The greatest natural desire of her heart was to be married and raise a family. And yet never once did I see her allow those desires to manipulate her choices or her emotions. When she was single, she lived radiantly and joyfully for the kingdom of God. She poured out her life in service to the least, the lonely, and the outcast. She spent time daily in God's presence, worshipping

Him and meditating on who He is. And she followed His leading for her life without first evaluating if her steps of obedience would bring her closer to marriage. She desired marriage. But she desired Jesus Christ even more.

Through Krissy's example, I learned how to surrender even my specific emotions toward specific guys back to Christ. When a guy came into my life I found myself attracted to, I learned not to panic about it. God showed me that it was normal and natural for me to feel drawn to certain guys—especially if they were godly examples of Christ.

It was not wrong to have the feelings. But it was crucial that the feelings didn't have *me*.

I began to practice surrendering my feelings of attraction into God's hands. Rather than obsess or fantasize about a guy, I learned how to pray for him and for his future wife. If I ever found that those emotions and desires started consuming me, I prayed for unsaved loved ones or meditated on Scripture in order to "take every thought captive" and not allow my feelings to distract me from Jesus Christ. The more I put this principle into practice, the more it became habitual to submit my emotions and desires to Christ and not allow them to control me.

When Eric first came into my life, it seemed inconceivable that such an incredible, gifted, Christ-focused man—who was five years older than me—would ever be interested in me romantically. I was very drawn to him physically, emotionally, and spiritually. But I felt a strong caution from God's Spirit not to allow my attraction to take over and affect the way I interacted with him. I asked God to supernaturally enable me to view Eric as a friend and brother in Christ—and He did just that.

Though I still felt feelings of attraction toward Eric at times, I didn't become infatuated with him. He became a wonderful friend and encouragement in my walk with Christ, but I wasn't constantly wondering if he was going to be my husband someday. This ability did not come from my own willpower, but by the enabling grace of God.

In the past, as soon as I would encounter an attractive, godly guy, I would immediately become mentally and emotionally obsessed with him. That's the natural tendency of the female heart. Only the Spirit of God can give us what we need to overcome those temptations and be enslaved not to our emotions, but to Him alone.

Of course, when God made it clear that Eric and I were to pursue a relationship leading toward marriage, I was free to let my emotions, desires, and attraction toward him blossom, under God's guidance. Bringing my natural desires under the control of God's Spirit did not diminish romance and passion in my relationship with Eric. Rather, saving those things for their proper context made them more exciting and beautiful.

Just because you choose to seek fulfillment in Christ rather than pursuing an earthly love story doesn't mean you'll lose your desire to be married. And when attractive godly men come your way, it's natural that you will be drawn to some of them. This doesn't mean that you've lost your contentment in Christ. It just means you are a woman, feeling the intrinsic desire for love and companionship that God placed in your heart. Feelings and emotions don't dictate or lessen your commitment to Christ, unless you allow those feelings and emotions to take over and control you, or distract you from your first love.

Hannah Whitehall Smith said it well:

> Do not be troubled by it. It is only in your emotions, and is not worth a moment's thought. Only see to it that your will is in God's hands, that your inward self is abandoned to His working, and that your choice, your decision is on His side; and there leave it. Your surging emotions, like a tossing vessel at anchor, which by degrees yields to the steady pull of the cable, finding themselves attached to the mighty power of God by the choice of your will, must inevitably come into captivity, and give their allegiance to Him.[5]

I once spoke to a beautiful thirtysomething single woman named Sara who said that even though she was fully content in her singleness and fully satisfied in Christ, she still experienced loneliness from time to time. "I don't see loneliness as a bad thing," she told me. "I see it as a wonderful chance to draw closer to Jesus Christ. I take my loneliness to God. I ask Him to comfort me and strengthen me. And He always does! He is the One who said, 'I will not leave you as orphans; I will come to you.' Every time I've cried out to Him in my loneliness, He draws near...and in His presence is fullness of joy."

Attraction, desire, emotions, loneliness—all of these things will surely come. But if we remain yielded to our Lord above all else, those things will never threaten our consecration to Him. They will only provide opportunities to experience His tenderness, faithfulness, and comfort in an ever-increasing way.

Here's what a Christ-focused single young woman told me recently about giving her desires back to God:

> If I see a guy that meets the spiritual standards of integrity that I look for, I tell God about him, not the guy himself, and oftentimes not even my friends! I don't allow my mind to daydream about guys in my life or to build castles in the sky over someone I think might be the one. I surrender my emotions and trust God to fulfill His purposes for me. This sometimes can be pretty hard, but that's where the promises of Scripture have made a huge difference, as well as avoiding most romantic movies! As the verse goes, "I have set the LORD always before me; because he is at my right hand, I shall not be moved" (Psalm 16:8).

This is a beautiful illustration of having the desire to be married, yet not allowing that desire to have *you*!

Overcoming Self-Pity
Jessica's Story
(age 21)

I will never forget receiving the wedding invitation from one of my best friends. I really wanted to be happy for her; she was marrying her boyfriend of several years. Weddings are usually joyous, happy occasions. But for the single woman who is sitting there watching the dreams of her friend being fulfilled, it can be painful! I remember sitting through the ceremony, experiencing overwhelming feelings of loneliness as I watched her exchange vows with the one she loved.

When will that special man come into my life? When will all heads turn to watch me walk down the isle in a beautiful wedding gown? Thoughts like these kept crowding into my mind. It did not help matters when another friend, who had promised to make the cakes for my wedding, approached me at the reception with the question, "So, will we be hearing news about a wedding for you anytime soon?"

With a tone of sadness I replied, "I don't know."

Then she hit me with the follow-up question, "Is there a special young man in your life?"

I muttered, "No, not at the moment."

At that point she felt compelled to offer this warning, "Don't wait until I'm in a wheelchair and can't bake cakes anymore!" She went on her way, leaving me feeling miserable and forsaken.

About two months later, the Lord spoke to my heart and convicted me of my feelings of discontentment and selfishness. He reminded me that He is all that I need, and nothing should change that fact. He showed me that this season of singleness has been determined by Him according to His plan for my life. He urged me to use this time to grow in my relationship with Him.

The Lord gently showed me that while wallowing in my self-pity, I was missing many great opportunities to serve others! As I meditated on God's Word and the things He spoke to my heart, I felt the chains fall off. Yes, I had been in bondage; a self-imposed bondage of misery and loneliness. But I was now free, with a new attitude and a renewed purpose and direction. Seek to draw close to my Lord daily, serve Him by serving others, and glorify Him through my life! I realized what a truly amazing opportunity He had given me.

A few months later when at a friend's bridal shower, someone asked me, "So, are you ready to be married?" I answered with complete honesty, "Right now, I am content where I am." James 1:17 says, "Every good gift and every perfect gift is from above." Singleness is a good and perfect gift from God for my life at this time. As I seek Him, daily I find that He really is all that I need.

Psalm 107:9 says, "He satisfies the longing soul, and fills the hungry soul with goodness." Over and over again, I have seen this promise ring true in my life. Of all of the delights and pleasures that this world has to offer, I have found that there is nothing and no one who can truly satisfy like Jesus. We were created with a void that only Jesus is meant to fill. And while I am looking forward to enjoying the relationship and companionship of my future husband, to put my life on hold until God brings him into my life is meaningless. Jesus Christ is the only One who can give me eternal joy, satisfaction, and fulfillment. He and He alone is more than enough for me! There are so many people who need to hear the life-changing message of the Gospel. Sharing Christ with others indeed brings true joy and contentment.

In my quiet times with the Lord I often read in Matthew 25:40, where the Lord says to His disciples, "Inasmuch as you did it to one of the least of these My brethren, you did it to Me." Choosing to forget about myself, and invest in the lives of others is motivated by the knowledge that Christ is glorified. This others-centered perspective not only leaves me feeling fulfilled and content, but I am also left with the joy of knowing that when my actions and attitudes help others, I am ultimately doing it unto Christ.

The Lord has opened the door for me to minister to troubled teen girls and children. In our ministry area there are numerous problems, including crime, drug and alcohol sale and use, prostitution, teen pregnancies, and child neglect. God has given me the privilege of sharing the love of Christ and the wonderful message of the Gospel. Despite the hard life circumstances, many of the teen girls and children of this community have made the choice to give their lives to Jesus. It is a blessing to disciple them, watch them grow in their faith, and to see them make choices that can lead them out of the troubled life circumstances in which they presently live. The pleasures of being used by God to be a blessing to others cannot be put into words. The happiness and joy that come as a result of choosing to put others first can in no way compare to the temporary delight of focusing and concentrating on myself.

My Encouragement to My Single Sisters

I would encourage any young woman who desires to be used by God for His glory to first and foremost have an attitude of surrender. The Lord has an amazing plan for each life and He desires for us to be surrendered to His lordship and available for use in any way He desires. I challenge you to keep your eyes on Jesus, the Author and Finisher of our faith, and not to get distracted or grow discontent in your singleness. God is a sovereign and faithful Father who loves you more than you can imagine and yearns for an intimate relationship with you. I would exhort you to choose now in your single years to cultivate a deep, intimate relationship with the Lord, and to fall in love with Jesus, so that your life will be a vessel of honor fit for the Master's use.

8

Doesn't God Want Me to Be Happy?
Understanding God's Heart for Singleness

*I'm afraid the snake has been talking to [many of us]. He's
been sneaking up and whispering, "God is stingy. He dangles
that beautiful fruit called marriage before your eyes and
won't let you have it. He refuses you the only thing you need
for deep personal growth, the one thing in all the world that
would solve all your problems and make you really happy."*

ELISABETH ELLIOT

There's a clever little lie floating around out there today. It appeals to our fleshly, selfish side, and whispers words such as: *Singleness is not a gift, and God never intended us to accept it as such. Most of us are miserable being single—we might as well admit it! Singleness can't really be a gift from God because it's not fun, and of course He wants us to be happy.*

One of the books I quoted from earlier takes this position:

> Singleness is a "gift," at least that's what we've been taught.
> But if singleness is a gift, then why does it make us feel so
> miserable so often? Does God really want his children to
> embrace a gift they resent so much?...I don't know about you,
> but for me being single just got worse and worse. I didn't
> become the "dynamic" single that Christian books promised
> me I could be. Instead of reaching some sort of "singleness
> nirvana" I realized I was being tricked into denying my very
> self by pretending to be happy with single life.[1]

Self-Denial vs. Self-Fulfillment

The author, in the quote above, claims she was "being tricked into denying [her] very self." Think about that for a minute. Was Christ trying to "trick" us when He said, "If anyone desires to come after Me, *let him deny himself*, and take up his cross, and follow Me"? (Matthew 16:24, emphasis added).

Once again, American Christianity tells us to exalt our emotions and desires above the call of Christ to die to self, lay all our dreams and hopes on the altar, and take up our cross daily. After all, how could a loving God expect us to embrace something that makes us resentful and miserable? Why would God want us to surrender our desire to be married when clearly it is a *good* desire? How ludicrous to receive singleness as a gift! It's only natural that we remain impatient and discontent until we are finally married—because that's what God wants for us. He wants us to be happy. And marriage is the only way to be happy, according to this view.

The message "hurry up and get married already" caters to what *we* want. It's all about following the whims and desires of our heart. If our heart says that we are lonely and need to get married to solve our loneliness, then that must be what God wants for us. After all, He's a God of love!

But this very same loving God asked His only Son to embrace the greatest suffering this world has ever known. Hebrews 12:2 tells us that Christ *endured* the cross, *despising the shame*. It was not easy and comfortable for Jesus to give up His life. It was not delightful and pleasant. Taking up His cross caused Him more pain and misery than anyone has ever known or imagined. It was so difficult that the night before it happened He wept exceedingly, sweat drops of blood, and cried out to His father, *"Is there any other way?"*

What if Jesus had simply listened to His "heart" that night in the Garden of Gethsemane? What if He had taken that particular book's advice and yielded to what His emotions and human desires were telling Him? What if He had said, "Surely God does not want me to embrace something that makes me feel so miserable? Surely

I shouldn't see this as an opportunity from My Father! Death is a curse. It's shameful; it's painful. Why would I surrender to something that doesn't make *Me* feel happy?"

Precious sisters, let us never profane the sacred sacrifice of our King by seeking the benefits of Christ without the cross! Just as He gave up His life, so we are called to give up ours. It doesn't matter what makes us happy or what makes us feel good. Yes, the way is narrow and rocky and causes us pain, but that's the very road Jesus walked—and may it be our greatest privilege and joy to follow in His steps.

As I've said before, on the other side of sacrifice is always joy. Jesus obtained the reward of His suffering after He had conquered sin and death, and sat down on the right hand of His Father. That's His pattern. First suffering—then reward. As 1 Peter 5:10 says, "May the God of all grace, who called us to His eternal glory by Christ Jesus, *after you have suffered a while*, perfect, establish, strengthen, and settle you" (emphasis added). And Paul reminds us, "God is not unjust to forget your work and labor of love" (Hebrews 6:10). When we lay our all on the altar, no matter how painful the process is, we can be confident that there are unspeakable treasures of joy awaiting us on the other side of the suffering.

Modern messages on "shedding the stigma of singleness" tell us that embracing singleness as a gift only causes resentment and misery. But no suffering that we embrace in obedience to Jesus Christ ever ends in misery and death. That wasn't Jesus' story, and it won't be our story when we follow in His steps. God specializes in happily ever after. Just read the end of the Bible and you'll see what I mean.

Like I've said, the majority of Christian single young women today are surrounded by messages that encourage them to follow their hearts, take matters into their own hands, and find themselves a husband as quickly as possible. If that is your situation, I would strongly encourage you to tune out those noisy voices and lean upon the strength of God to walk a different path—His path. Remember

Jesus in the Garden of Gethsemane. The cross seemed too much to bear. But He received everything He needed by running into the arms of His Father and crying out for supernatural strength.

He will do the same for you. All you must to do is ask.

Honesty or Sin?

Another misconception being promoted under the banner of "just be honest" Christianity is the message that it is literally impossible to be happy or content in your singleness (unless you are one of the few called to lifelong Biblical celibacy). Those who hold this view say that anyone claiming to be content in their singleness is just pretending.

Here's how a book I quoted from earlier says it:

> I am always amazed by women who [say things like]: "No, I'm not really looking for a significant relationship right now. I'm really growing in the Lord right now, and I'm so happy/content/secure in my relationship with Him..." While some of us may wonder if it's possible to reach such a place of peaceful acceptance (what I like to call singleness nirvana—that state rumored to be out there somewhere but that doesn't really exist), many of us walk away mumbling, "Oh, come on!" under our breaths. When single women tell me how wonderfully happy they are being single, I'm left [thinking that] it doesn't ring true. We must be honest with ourselves—and each other—if we are ever going to change things. Maybe you are not ready to stand up at the next singles event at church and admit that you are...ticked off that you're not having sex. I understand if you're not there yet. Few women are ready for such a level of self-disclosure![2]

There is a disturbing trend in modern Christianity that says it's more spiritual to "just be honest" with our struggles and frustrations, like this author who implies that it would be great if only we had the guts to stand up and publicly admit we are fed up with being single and "ticked off that [we are] not having sex."

But I believe this kind of "honesty" is nothing more than a slap in God's face. It's a flaunting of the flesh—that whining, selfish, demanding side of us that constantly wars against God's Spirit.

No matter what our situation in life, we should not go around being "ticked off" about it. Rather, God tells us in 1 Thessalonians 5:18, "In everything give thanks; for this is the will of God in Christ Jesus concerning you." And in Philippians 2:14, "Do all things without complaining and disputing."

If we are feeling angry, unhappy, miserable, or ticked off about being single (or any other circumstance in life), we shouldn't merely admit it and call it honesty. Rather, we should admit it and call it what it is—sin. We should ask God to forgive us and cleanse us by the power of His blood. And we should lean upon His grace to turn and walk another way, joyfully embracing whatever path God has placed us on, just like Jesus, who endured the cross.

No, this is not over-spiritualizing singleness. It's applying the Gospel to singleness.

In *Authentic Beauty* I wrote about Corrie ten Boom being challenged by God to give thanks for the fleas that infested her prison cell. She told her sister, "Betsy, there is no way that even God can make me thankful for a flea." But once she began rejoicing in the fleas, she soon found that these annoying little insects truly *were* a gift from God. The guards were so disgusted by them that they avoided going to check the sisters' prison cell every night. Betsy and Corrie were free to read their Bible, pray, sing, and witness to other prisoners—something that would have been impossible had the guards come to check their cell. It was like a little taste of heaven on earth, and it would not have been possible without the fleas.

Paul makes it clear in 1 Corinthians that singleness presents an unmatched *opportunity*:

> I say to the unmarried and to the widows: It is good for them to remain even as I am...I want you to be without care. He who is unmarried cares for the things of the Lord—how he may please the Lord. But he who is married cares about the things of the world—how he may please his wife...The unmarried woman cares about the things of the Lord, that she may be holy both in body and in spirit. But she who is married cares about the things of the world—how she may please her husband. And this I say for your own profit, not that I may put a leash on you, but for what is proper, and that you may serve the Lord without distraction...So then he who [marries] does well, but he who does not [marry] does better...A wife is bound by law as long as her husband lives; but if her husband dies, she is at liberty to be married to whom she wishes, only in the Lord. But she is happier if she remains as she is, according to my judgment—and I think I also have the Spirit of God (1 Corinthians 7:8, 32-35,39-40).

If you read the entire passage, you'll see that Paul goes out of his way to make it clear that those who marry are not sinning. However, he also goes out of his way to say that singleness, whether for a season or a lifetime, is a wonderful chance to serve the Lord without distraction. He even goes so far as to say that a woman who loses her husband will be *happier* if she remains single than if she gets married again. As Paul clearly points out, he does not prescribe this path in order to put a leash upon us, or make us miserable, *but for our benefit*. There are unspeakable joys and treasures in a season or lifetime of singleness that we miss out on when we look to marriage as our source of happiness. Paul is so content and fulfilled in his single life with Christ that he wishes all men were as himself!

The modern voices we've been discussing disagree that Paul is saying singleness is a good thing. Some contend that Paul was speaking specifically to people in that particular time period, and his advice stemmed from the fact that they were in the midst of a great crisis of famine (which by the way, cannot be biblically proven).

It is dangerous to start using the "time period" argument. Pretty soon the entire Bible can be downplayed because it was "written for a different time." It's far safer to build upon the words of 2 Timothy 3:16: "*All Scripture* is given by inspiration of God, and is profitable for doctrine, for reproof, for correction, for instruction in righteousness."

Others argue that Paul himself admitted that he spoke these things "by permission" (1 Corinthians 7:6 KJV) and not command. I do not feel we should take this portion of Scripture less seriously because of that one sentence. As far as I (and countless scholars throughout history) am concerned, it's still the Word of God. But even if you *do* take the position that these verses are merely Paul's personal opinion and not the inspired Word of God, think about this: Wouldn't you rather take the personal advice of Paul—who, when he *was* under divine inspiration said, "Imitate me, just as I also imitate Christ" (1 Corinthians 11:1)—over any modern-day Christian's thoughts on the subject?

The bottom line is this: Singleness *is* a gift, an opportunity, and a blessing, and it should be treated as such. That doesn't mean we should swear off marriage. That doesn't mean the desire to be married is wrong. And that doesn't mean we should stop praying that God would bring our spouse into our life in His own time and way.

But it *does* mean we should stop griping and complaining about singleness and that we should allow God to reveal His amazing purposes for this season of our lives. Often, He will delay bringing marriage into our life until we've learned to find perfect contentment in Him. It's the same with ministry opportunities, children, and other dreams and desires He's placed in our hearts. The dreams themselves are good and God given, but keeping a death grip on them is not.

If you have been griping and complaining (even just inwardly) about being single, ask God to forgive you and wash you clean. Ask Him to enable you by the power of His grace to be truly thankful for this gift of singleness (and yes, according to Paul, it *is* a gift!) and to more clearly see His divine purpose for this season of your life. Entrust your desire for marriage to Him. There is no safer place for your hopes and dreams than in the loving hands of your faithful Father. When He holds the pen, He can and will write a beautiful story for you, both in your single years, and, if He so ordains, in your earthly love story.

And by the way, this process doesn't just apply to the area of singleness! I'm constantly being convicted of areas that I've inwardly been whining about, wallowing in discontentment "until such-and-such finally happens." Paul says that when we learn to do all things without complaining, we will become *blameless and pure* in the midst of a crooked and perverse generation (Philippians 2:14-15). It's no small command—and no small promise!

Part Three

Living a Poured-Out Life

A Sacred Season Awaits!

9

The Sacred Opportunity of Singleness
Learning to Look Beyond Self

*One of the keys to being fulfilled and content is to be others-centered.
When you live a poured-out life, you realize you aren't the only one
struggling or going through a hard time or waiting on the promises
of God to be fulfilled in your life. It is hard for me to think about
myself when there is a family living in a mud hut that has no food
to eat and no bed to sleep in. It is hard for me to think about my
dreams when I am comforting a child who has just lost her mother
to AIDS. It is hard for me to think about my desires when I live with
75 orphans who know the pain of rejection and abandonment.*
KARRIS, 28-YEAR-OLD SINGLE MISSIONARY

*Learning to be others-centered is a massive cure for any type of
ailment...lovesickness, single-sickness, depression, or anything else. For
it is when we take our eyes off our own inadequacies and losses that we
are truly able to be used for others. And as we are used to help others,
our pain slowly goes away. (You can't focus on two things at once!)*
MELODY, 32-YEAR-OLD SINGLE NURSE

Lydia was a beautiful, intelligent woman in her mid-thirties. A gifted teacher from Denmark, she had a thriving career and a seemingly perfect life. Her family was wealthy and respected, and she had recently become engaged to an attractive and successful man.

But something was missing from Lydia's life. Inwardly, there was an inexplicable need for more. She had everything the world could offer, so why did she feel empty and unfulfilled?

In desperation she began to wonder about God. She had never been a religious person, but for some reason she felt that maybe He was what was missing from her life. Lydia didn't know any Christians, so she realized she would have to find out about God on her own. She pulled a dusty Bible from her bookshelf and began reading it. Night after night she spent hours at her kitchen table, drinking coffee, smoking cigarettes, and pouring over the Scriptures. After several weeks, her heart was open and ready. She knew this was the truth. And she knew she must surrender her life to this God who had died to rescue her.

Everything in Lydia's life changed. Her addiction to alcohol and cigarettes was broken. Her love for late-night parties and concerts faded. Her desire for wealth and success was replaced by a longing to pour herself out for the least around the world. And her desire for marriage changed into an intense longing for intimacy with Jesus Christ.

Much to the astonishment of her family and friends, Lydia broke things off with her money-loving fiancé, walked away from her successful career, and gave all of the money in her savings account to a missionary who was starting an orphan's home in Africa. And for months she sought God and prayed about where she was to go, what she was to do.

Out of all the things Lydia laid upon the altar during that season, giving up her prospects for marriage was the most difficult. Already in her mid-thirties, she knew that "time was running out" if she ever wanted to settle down and build a nest. But God was calling her to a life of radical abandonment to Him, and she trusted that He would be more than enough to sustain and fulfill her, even if He never brought a man into her life.

After a year of prayer, Lydia felt strongly that God wanted her to go to Jerusalem as a missionary of the Gospel. With very little money and no real contacts there, Lydia set off, trusting that God would meet her every need. She ended up in a tiny basement apartment, praying and wondering why God had called her to this strange place.

A few days later, there was a knock on her door. A man stood there with a deathly ill baby in his arms. "We cannot take care of her," he said. "She will probably die soon, but will you take her anyway?"

Baffled, Lydia took the child and laid her on the bed. The apartment was bitterly cold. There was no milk or food or blankets. There were no doctors or hospitals around. The streets were dangerous. Raids and attacks were common. No one ever ventured out at night. How could she possibly keep this little girl alive?

Crying out to God, Lydia prayed over the sick child, asking for a miracle. Many times during the night, Lydia thought the baby had died. But in the morning, she was still alive—and even looked a bit better. Soon it was evident that God had answered her prayers and performed a miracle.

That was the beginning of the amazing ministry God had called Lydia to. The child became her own daughter. She began to pour out her life in service to the sick, the orphaned, the poor, the dying, the fearful, and the oppressed people of Jerusalem. She learned how to lean upon God for every need, for every meal, for every problem. God continued to bring needy children to Lydia's doorstep. Within a few years, she was a mother to ten little ones. She didn't have the natural resources to provide for them or keep them healthy. But God did, and never once did any of them go without.

Lydia had given up expecting to get married. She certainly did not live in a place that was conducive to finding a husband. But she had no intention of changing her direction, because she knew she was exactly where God wanted her. He was more than a Husband to her every single day. And He had beautifully blessed her life with many precious children. Through her obedience to her Lord, her dream of motherhood had come true. She was joyful, fulfilled, and content.

One day a missionary and Bible student named Derek came across Lydia's path. He was just visiting Jerusalem for a short while. He never expected to meet someone like Lydia there. But when he began to observe her work and ministry, he was baffled. He'd never seen a woman like her—or even conceived that a woman like this existed. Here is how Derek described Lydia's impact upon him:

> Having graduated in Britain from Eton College and Cambridge University, I had at that time held a fellowship at King's College, Cambridge for six years. But a completely new phase of my education began the day I climbed the outside stairs of a gray stone house and met the blue-eyed Danish woman whom a houseful of Jewish and Arab children called Mama. In that house I met the Holy Spirit, not as one Person of a theological doctrine called the Trinity, but as a present, potent, daily reality. I watched Lydia set out plates on the table when there was no food to put on those plates, knowing that by the time we sat down to eat, God would have provided the meal. I watched her rebuke fever and sickness in the children and saw the sickness depart. Above all, I watched the Spirit nourish her, lead her, and support her all day, every day, through the pages of the Bible. I had studied the Scriptures in their original languages, analyzed their historic components, pondered their exegesis. Lydia let them speak to her heart. "I read the Gospel of John," she once said, "like a love letter." In thirty years of marriage I have learned from Lydia that prayer that springs from this kind of intimacy with the Bible is not a subjective thing, but a force in the world—the most powerful force there is.[1]

Derek and Lydia were married and raised nine adopted children together, serving and laboring for the kingdom of God. Obviously from Derek's own words, Lydia's beautiful intimacy with her Lord continued to make an impact upon him throughout their marriage.

Derek and Lydia's romance was a beautiful, God-scripted love story completely free of human strategy or manipulation. Their life was a spectacular display of God's glory and faithfulness, an amazing daily adventure with their King. And it would not have been possible if Lydia had clung to her own comforts and pursuits. She never would have met Derek or had the privilege of raising those children if she had stayed away from the mission field in the hopes of meeting the right guy; if she had put her life on hold until God brought a man across her path.

Lydia took up her cross and followed her King wherever He led. Her life was immensely blessed, though also immensely challenging.

Are you willing to take up the same challenge? Or are you determined to walk an easy road, one that is predictable, comfortable, and self-glorifying?

I hope that by the end of this chapter, you will have fully embraced Lydia's version of singleness. She did not have a special call upon her life. Rather, she was simply living out the very same call God has placed upon each one of us who claim to know Him—utter abandonment to His purposes and absolute trust in His faithfulness.

If you are single, God has a much higher calling upon your life than spending all your time and energy trying to snag Mr. Right. As Paul wrote, being unmarried is an amazing opportunity to serve the Lord without distraction. It's true that you might find a decent Christian guy by reading books with tips on how to get noticed or by joining an Internet dating service. But what a great adventure you will miss out on! What romance, beauty, and glory we forgo when we try to script the story ourselves.

God has not called us to build our lives around the pursuit of our own selfish desires, but to be poured-out sacrifices for His kingdom. One of the great tragedies of American Christian young women is our total preoccupation with self. In my book *Set-Apart Femininity* I wrote about the dangers of the popular self-esteem message for women, which teaches that our own heart is good and encourages us to live to our true self and inhabit our own beauty. Not only is this a nonbiblical concept (we have no true eternal beauty outside of the beauty of Jesus Christ, and we only bring Him glory by *dying* to self, not living to it), but the real danger is that it keeps us consumed with *me, me, me* while the rest of the world is sick and oppressed and dying and impoverished. We in America are wealthy and comfortable beyond what most people in the world can even imagine. In the single season of life, we are freer than we'll ever be to give our lives to those in need and become Christ's advocates for the least around the world.

But we don't use our advantage for that cause. Instead we sit around complaining about petty concerns and evaluating our own emotions. We attend retreats that are all about how we can feel better about ourselves and live more fulfilled lives. We read books about how we can somehow find the right guy. We spend hours online frittering our time away in endless social networks. We waste countless hours at the mall, snatching up the latest trends and trying to become more appealing to the opposite sex. We live a life completely focused on self. Meanwhile, children are starving, women are being prostituted, and countless families around the world are ripped apart by disease and poverty.

In your single years, more than ever, you have the ability to give your life for them; to pour out your time, your energy, your love, and your resources to those that have God's special favor...the poor. Are you using this gift for the benefit of those in need, or are you squandering it on yourself?

Remember the evil city of Sodom in the Old Testament? The one that was destroyed by God's fury with fire and brimstone? Few of us are aware that God was angry for something beyond just immorality. As it says in Ezekiel:

> This was the iniquity of your sister Sodom: She and her daughter had pride, fullness of food, and abundance of idleness; neither did she strengthen the hand of the poor and needy (Ezekiel 16:49).

I don't know about you, but to me that description couldn't fit American Christianity any better. We are proud, focused on self, consumed with our wealth and comforts; we live in an abundance of idleness and shallow pleasure; and we are indifferent to the plight of the needy around the world. And once you see the end of Sodom, it makes you a bit uncomfortable to realize that America is on the very same path.

So I challenge you today to evaluate the direction of your life, remembering that it is not your own, and that it has been bought with a price with the very blood of Christ. If you have read my book *Set-Apart Femininity*, you might remember the chapter about the sacred claim that God has upon the life of every young women who yields her existence to Him. Here is how I explained it in that book:

> When we partake of holy communion, we are not just remembering what Christ did for us. We are stating to our Master that through this covenant, our body and blood are His to spend as He chooses. His body and blood for us. *Our body and blood for Him.*
>
> Paul says, "Do you not know that your bodies are members of Christ?" (1 Corinthians 6:15). We are the body of Christ. We are His hands and feet. What do Christ's hands and feet do? They bind wounds. They offer forgiveness. They set captives free. They heal the sick. They minister to children. They seek out the sinner. They drive out evil from the temple of God. They walk the road to Calvary. And they are pierced through that we might be saved.
>
> If you have chosen the set-apart path of a woman who fears the Lord, your life is not your own. The Spirit of Christ has a claim upon you. You have a call upon your life; you have a job to do. He has called you to minister His love to those in need. This sacred claim is the highest privilege we could ever receive. We can never repay what Christ did for us on the Cross. But because He has made us His hands and feet to this world, we have the incredible opportunity to give to others the very same astounding, transforming love that He gave to us.[2]

So how do we respond to such a high calling? My first challenge to you is to dedicate your singles years (and all the years beyond, but it starts with where you are at today) to be poured out for the glory of Christ. Are you willing to lay all your own pursuits upon the altar and allow Him to make your body a living sacrifice? This is not a decision to take lightly. This is not just something that should be theoretical in your life. This decision will very likely require a radical shift in direction; a painful letting go of comforts and dreams. And it may very well mean that you must forgo your constant striving to find an earthly prince in exchange for a more "hidden" life of sacrificial service to Christ. It may mean becoming far less "available" for guys to notice you, and far more available for Jesus Christ's purposes. This commitment may call you to a remote village in Africa, or an orphanage in Haiti, or an inner-city slum. God's sacred claim may ask you to pour your life out for one special-needs child or give your life to rescue hundreds of enslaved child prostitutes.

Karris is a beautiful twenty-eight-year-old single woman who has poured out her life for the orphans of Haiti for the past six years. She recently shared with me about how God has challenged her to lay down the pursuit of marriage in order to become a living sacrifice for Jesus Christ. Here is what she said:

> One of my greatest dreams in life has been to get married. I can remember being a young girl and praying for my future husband. I was almost 100 percent positive I would be married young, at 19 or 20 years old. A few weeks ago, I was looking through one of my journals and found this entry from June 23, 1998, "Right now I am 17 and I want to get married soon—probably by 20 years old." Looking back, I think of how God was just smiling at me. I am glad He did not choose to tell me that I would still be single ten years later! As every year passed, I began to realize God was asking me to lay down my dreams in order to accomplish His purpose in my life. I wanted to attend a university right after high school, but when it came time to turn in

my acceptance form, I did not have peace. I tried to brush it off, thinking it was just me, but as time went on, I knew the Lord was asking me to lay down that dream, stay at home, work, and go to a local community college. Finally, I chose to lay down that dream.

Paul says in Philippians 4:12, "I have learned the secret of being content" (NIV). I believe that secret is finding fulfillment in Jesus Christ. So many young people put their lives "on hold" while waiting for the right guy or girl to come along. Growing up, I always wanted to be a missionary. I wanted to go into the worst areas and show people the love of God. I thought I would get married first and then go out into the world, but God had a different plan. I sometimes wonder, "What if I had put my life on hold until I met the right guy?" I would have never gone to Haiti. Although there are hard times and lonely nights, I have found the secret of being content…. finding fulfillment in Jesus Christ.

I moved to Haiti in September 2002, and I have seen the faithfulness and provision of the Lord in so many ways. He has been my Provider. He has been my comfort on lonely nights. He has given me wisdom when I needed it the most. He has cared about every detail of my life. He has been my best friend, Father, and Husband all in one.

There are many nights I go to bed in tears, not because of sadness, but because of an overwhelming love for God and for what He has called me to do. I have said to God a number of times, "Thank You for not sending me my husband when I wanted it. What I would have looked to an earthly husband to fulfill in my life, You have been that for me and more."

I believe all of us are missionaries. You do not have to move to Haiti to be a missionary. You can be one in your high school. You can be one in the college you are attending. You can be one while working in the corporate world. I try to advance the kingdom of God wherever I am, in whatever situation. The Bible says in 1 Corinthians 7:34, "An unmarried woman or virgin is concerned about the Lord's affairs: Her aim is to be devoted to the Lord in both body and spirit. But a married woman is concerned about the affairs of this world—how she can please her husband" (NIV). As a single woman, this verse is an encouragement to me. This clearly states that our single years are crucial years because we can be completely devoted to the Lord and be used in a mighty way to advance His kingdom.

The Best Way to Find a Guy

As odd as it may sound, I believe the best way to find a godly marriage partner is to stop hunting for one and instead focus your entire life around Jesus Christ and His priorities. We should never put off fulfilling God's calling upon our life because we haven't met our man yet. As Lydia's story demonstrates, God is not limited by our circumstances or surroundings.

If He wants you to be married, He is more than capable of bringing a man into your life in the most unlikely way, in the most unlikely place. God can bring your spouse to you in the remotest village in Africa or in the most hidden slum of Haiti. Or, like Krissy, He can bring your man along even in rural Michigan, where the only available men seemed to be elderly widowers! Lydia and Krissy are just two of many amazing testimonies I've encountered of women who didn't put their life's calling on hold until they met their man, but willingly followed the call of God on their lives and became active in work for His kingdom—even though it meant being less available to the opposite sex. And, amazingly, it was in a place of seeming obscurity that God wrote their love stories and brought along their husbands.

Remember that there are many Christ-built warrior-poet men out there who are praying and hoping for a set-apart young women— one who is not following after the trends of the culture, one who is not wallowing around in discontentment or on the prowl for a guy. Nothing would thrill a true warrior-poet's heart more than to know that his future bride was spilling her life out for the sake of the Gospel. Want to find a godly guy? Focus on pouring your life out for Jesus Christ and leave the rest to Him. As it says in Psalm 57:2, He will be more than faithful to fulfill His purposes for you.

How to Make the Shift

God can transform a discontent, worried, anxious, guy-consumed single young woman into a vibrant, radiant, fulfilled soldier of the cross. If you feel far from a triumphant attitude right now, don't despair. Making Jesus Christ your all in all isn't something you can accomplish in your own strength. You need the supernatural enabling power of God to overtake you and equip you to live a life you never could have lived on your own.

If you are ready to make a shift in your focus and begin dedicating your life, not to the pursuit of a guy, but to the pouring out of your life for those Christ loves, then simply come to Him and tell Him so. Get alone with your King and consecrate your body as a living sacrifice unto His purposes from this day forward. Ask Him to fill you with His Spirit and supernaturally equip you to shift your focus from finding an earthly romance to being so caught up in Him that nothing else matters. Ask Him to reveal to you any activities or habits in your life that are not glorifying to Him. Ask Him to show you anything in your life, as harmless as it might seem, that is distracting you from having a single-minded focus on your Savior. And then, by His grace, remove each and every one of those stumbling blocks from your existence.

Next, take some time to prayerfully consider the direction and focus of your life. What is God calling you to? How can you respond to the sacred claim He has upon your existence? How can you practically become His hands and feet to this lost and dying world? Ask Him to open your eyes and show you what next steps to take.

And remember, it might be necessary to make a complete shift in your life direction. American mentalities train us that this life is all about our dreams, our goals, and our ambitions. But that's not true Christianity. How might God be asking you to forsake all, take up your cross, and follow Him? (I will offer some practical ideas in the next chapter.)

There is a dire and desperate need all around us. Millions and millions of people around the world are facing unspeakable suffering. They are living without hope and, even worse, dying without knowing Jesus. As Jackie Pullinger says, if we will not reach them with the love of Jesus Christ, who will?

Well-meaning modern voices declare that "marriage is a worthy goal worth pursuing." Marriage is certainly a worthy and God-given desire, but it should never become a goal we pursue with our life. Rather, a poured-out life for Jesus Christ is a worthy goal worth pursuing. A life that selflessly and sacrificially serves the least is a worthy goal worth pursuing. And a heart that trusts in Jesus Christ wholly and completely and surrenders the pen into His faithful and capable hands is a worthy goal worth pursuing.

Like Karris, ask God to shift your passions and desires from marriage to His sacred calling upon your life. You will never regret the glorious exchange. And if God's purpose for your life is marriage, you can trust that even your difficult steps of obedience to Jesus Christ will lead you closer to your earthly prince. That's the beauty of our Lord's ways.

10

Sisters of the Common Life
Real-Life Inspiration from Modern Single Women

*Remember the attitude, "Today, God has called me to be
content as a single. So today, I am going to be the happiest
single alive, and I am going to accomplish the most for
God that is possible, because He walks at my side!"*
MELODY, 32-YEAR-OLD SINGLE

You don't have to be amazingly gifted or highly educated to pour out your life for Jesus Christ and dedicate your single years to the "least of these." You don't have to have been seminary educated or groomed at Bible college. You just need a heart fully surrendered to Him. Gladys Aylward was an uneducated parlor maid when she set off, against the advice of the Christian system, to give her life to the people of China. Amy Carmichael was merely one simple girl in feeble health and with very few supporters when she left it all to rescue endangered children in India. Jackie Pullinger left home at age 20 to give her life for Jesus Christ with no real idea as to where she was going and with only about ten dollars to her name. All of these women changed the world for the Gospel. And it was not because of them. They were merely vessels willing to lay down everything for the kingdom of God.

Here are some real-life stories of single young women (some of them you have already met in this book) who are pouring their lives out for the least around the world. I hope you will be inspired by their journeys—and gain fresh vision for how God might want to do something similar through *your life*.

Karris' Story

Single Missionary to Haiti

When I was a little girl, we lived in Sacramento, California. My mom ran a storage center, where she would collect furniture, dishes, anything you could imagine, and we would deliver it to the poor and to the immigrants who were coming in. This was something I can remember doing on a weekly basis. So I grew up having a heart for the poor and needy. Whenever missionaries would come and speak at my church or school, I sat listening intently to every word. I loved the stories. I loved the adventure. I loved the idea of living a set-apart life for the Lord. I would read books on Mother Teresa and pray I would be able to reach out to the kinds of people she was reaching out to.

In my middle school years, I would always attend Christian summer camps. I was the one who was always at the altar, crying out to the Lord and asking Him to use me. Even at a young age, I knew there had to be more to the Christian life. When I was a teenager, I read the first book that Eric and Leslie Ludy had written. Their story made a huge impact in my life because it showed me what can happen when one truly decides to live a life set apart for the Lord.

When I began walking this path of living a set-apart life, one of my biggest challenges happened in my senior year of high school when I was deciding where to go to college. All of my friends were going away, and I figured it was the right thing to do. But I sensed that the Lord was telling me to lay down that desire and stay home that first year after high school. The thought of staying home, while all of my friends were off at school having fun, was depressing to me! Tearfully, I decided to obey the Lord. I did not turn in my enrollment form. Instead, I enrolled at a community college and worked two jobs. During that year, I remember crying a lot. It was a hard year. It was my first "real" experience of having to obey the Lord when it hurts. Obedience will ALWAYS require something of you.

One night, I remember sitting on my bed, crying to my mom and telling her how lonely I was. I was expecting to hear something like, "Its okay, Karris. I am so sorry you are going through this. You will come out of it." Instead, she said, "It is good you are experiencing this, because you now get to feel what most people feel."

During that year Pastor Bill Wilson from New York City came to speak at my church. I had always had a heart for the inner-city and he was the founder of the largest inner-city Sunday school in the world. I was 18 years old at the time, and I knew I had to go visit there. I went to their one-week boot camp program and then went through a four-month internship program. They asked me to come back on staff, so in 1999, I moved to Brooklyn, New York. I was there for three years and learned lifelong lessons about ministry, obedience, and sacrifice. While I was there, a lady named Danita Estrella came to visit. She had started an orphanage in Haiti. Danita moved to Haiti almost ten years ago with a promise from God, "Go, and I will be with you." The Lord did not tell her what she was going to be doing or that one day she would have a great ministry. He just gave her a promise and she obeyed. Her life was and is an example of a life truly set apart for Christ. The first time I met her, I gave her my paycheck that week for her orphanage, never knowing that a few years later I would be living there. When I heard Danita's stories, I was deeply touched. There was one about a little boy she was taking care of in a hospital who died. I was so overcome with emotion when I heard the stories of the children. The Lord had been preparing my heart to leave New York, but I did not know where I would be for the next season of my life. In 2002 a group of four of us went on a one-week mission trip to the orphanage in Haiti. After that week, I knew in my heart that I was "home." There was no doubt in my mind that the next season of my life would be spent as a missionary in Haiti. Six months later, I moved there. In September of this year, it will be seven years that I have been a part of Danita's Children (www.danitaschildren.org).

When I first moved there, the ministry was relatively small. All of us lived in one home with the 26 children in the orphanage. Our school had about 120 children. Our one building was a thatched structure in which we held our school, church, and feeding program! I have had the privilege of seeing the faithfulness of God as we have grown over the years. Presently, we have 75 children in the orphanage and more than 530 children in the school. The Lord has provided the funds for us to build a school, church, cafeteria, and an older boy's home. We are about to start the construction of a children's hospital, which is so desperately needed. My main role at Danita's Children is being the administrator. I handle the finances, receipts, payroll, etc. I love doing it because I can see the provision of God with my own eyes!

Over the years I have experienced joy and heartbreak. I have comforted mothers who have lost children. I have seen people die of AIDS. I have seen racism in the ugliest form. I have met a leper who was ostracized by her friends and family but decided to serve the Lord in the midst of her pain. I have had lonely nights. I have felt the pain of betrayal. On the other hand, I have seen lives changed by the power of love. I have looked at a child who was about to die and seen God turn their life around. I have been a part of rescuing 26 orphaned children from the floods of Gonaives. Proverbs 19:17 says, "He who is kind to the poor lends to the Lord, and he will reward him for what he has done" (NIV). This is the only verse that says we can actually lend something to the Lord. There are many nights in Haiti when I go to bed with tears in my eyes, thanking the Lord for the privilege of being able to serve the least of these. Who am I that God has chosen me?

I certainly won't say that being a single young woman has been easy. Sometimes I take my eyes off Christ, and that's when I start to struggle. I have seen my friends find the love of their life and get married, wondering when my turn will be. When I begin to think like that, my focus gets off of Christ. When I am in Haiti, I am thinking about others. It is hard to think about yourself when there are 75 children to take care of and kids dying of malnutrition all around me. When I come back to the States, I have to fight my flesh daily because I see others either with their boyfriends or husbands, and it is easy to get my eyes off of Christ.

Revelation 2:2-4 says, "I know your deeds, your hard work and your perseverance...you have persevered and have endured hardships for my name, and have not grown weary. Yet I hold this against you: You have forsaken your first love" (NIV). This verse has been so encouraging to draw me back whenever I get my eyes off of Christ. It is easy to be in the midst of ministry, yet forsaking your first love.

I am so thankful I decided to live a life set apart for Him. It is not always easy, but it is always worth it. There will be times when you will have to give up your dreams and desires, but the Lord will place within you His own dreams and His desires for your life.

There is a world out there that is suffering. There are people next to you who need to hear a kind word. There is someone nearby who is struggling because no one has reached out to them. There is a boy or girl who doesn't "fit in" with the popular group and cannot reach out on their own. Our mission field is wherever we are at the present moment. God might not call you to Haiti. He might not ask you to live in Africa or India or go work in the ghettos of New York. But He will ask you to do something. He will require you to give up what you want for what He wants.

I challenge you with the question today, "What is God requiring of you?" Are you willing to give up your will for His will? The beauty of that is the closer we get to God, the more we desire what He desires. He desires a life set apart. Do you?

Kelly's Story
Single Missionary to Inner-City Refugees

One of my greatest fears used to be the inner-city of Rochester, near where I live. Though Rochester is a wonderful place to live, there are certain areas that are some of the most dangerous in the country. All of my life, I have been told to avoid these areas.

Well-meaning Christian leaders had always stated, "There is no need for such a sweet girl like you to venture down there. You are not wanted there and are most likely to end up at the wrong place at the wrong time."

Did I really have to go down to the city? As I looked around my church, I realized I didn't see one poor person. As I observed my neighbors, I noticed that there were no orphans, no widows, no refugees. There were people just like me, healthy, comfortable, and well taken care of.

As I turned on the news, I saw what was happening in the inner-city. There were the poor. There were the needy and afflicted. There was an overwhelming population of refugees who were in great distress.

For months I contemplated if knowing Christ more really meant knowing the people whom I had avoided my entire life. The Word of God clearly stated yes.

The more I read the Word of God, the more convinced I felt. Jesus' definition of ministry was so drastically different from mine. The words of Christ I esteemed and loved had no trace or evidence within my own life.

Jesus' words kept ringing in my mind. "If you love Me, keep My commandments" (John 14:15).

I realized that my love for Christ was marked by beliefs rather than actions. I had to seek out the commands of my Lord Jesus. What did He desire that I pursue? Surely the abundant Christian life was more than just agreeing with truths. The love that my Lord desired was one marked by obedience.

In my search I came across this verse that radically altered my thinking. Jeremiah 22:16 says, "'He pled the cause of the afflicted and needy; then it was well. Is not that what it means to know Me?' declares the Lord" (NASB).

y knowledge of the Lord consisted of quiet times spent in

coffee shops with His Word. Did the Lord desire that I come to know Him through actions as well? An alarming thought crossed my mind. *If this verse is true, then I only partially know my Lord. There is still another half that I have yet to ever know or see!*

I had to dive deeper into the Scriptures to see what else the Lord had to say about pleading the cause of the afflicted and needy. Was this really a major theme in Scripture that I had flippantly passed by? I had spent hours in His Word—how could I have missed this?

David writes in the Psalms, "Defend the poor and fatherless; do justice to the afflicted and needy. Deliver the poor and needy; free them from the hand of the wicked" (Psalm 82:3).

Micah writes, "He hath shewed thee, O man, what is good; and what doth the Lord require of thee, but to do justly, and to love mercy, and to walk humbly with thy God?" (Micah 6:8 KJV).

Solomon wrote, "To do justice and judgment is more acceptable to the Lord than sacrifice" (Proverbs 21:3 KJV).

God's law commands in Leviticus, "But the stranger (refugee) that dwelleth with you shall be unto you as one born among you, and thou shalt love him as thyself" (Leviticus 19:34 KJV).

After reading these Scriptures the Spirit of God tugged on my heart. "Kelly, you need to leave this coffee shop in order to find the poor. You need to step foot into uncomfortable places to find the fatherless. Justice doesn't take place in coffee shops. It takes place on the front lines. You are sitting on the sidelines..."

At this point in the study I cried out, "My Lord, I do not know You fully because I do not know the poor, needy, and afflicted! Show them to me! I am desperate to know all of You!"

Little did I know at this moment what the Lord had in mind when I pleaded to know Him by knowing the afflicted.

I called up one of my friends and explained my great dilemma. She simply responded, "There are some people I want you to meet."

Over the next several months she took me to meet a group of people that has changed my life, refugees fleeing from genocide in Burma—the Karen people.

As I came to know these refugees an astounding thing happened. I also came to know my Lord Jesus even more by experience. As I ventured into the darkest places in the city, the principle, "The Lord is my shelter" was no longer theory; it was my reality.

Then something mysterious happened. I actually died to myself. Though I had claimed to die to self years earlier, there was no experience by which it would be tested. Yet as I have had to engage in work among the least of these, it is truly no longer I that live but Christ who lives in me.

I met Christ in the coffee shops. Christ met me among the least of these in the inner-city.

As a result the Lord has led me to start a nonprofit addressing the various needs of refugees, orphans, and widows. It is called the R.O.W. Project, and its simple mission is "to obey God's command to love, defend, and deliver the refugee, orphan, and widow."

We are in the process of establishing a center specifically designed for refugees in the Rochester area. This center will be a place where refugees can become empowered by the Word of God to build needed life skills and receive assistance with daily needs. The R.O.W. Project will be a place refugees can come for safety, learning, and rest. We then hope to send workers back to the refugees' home countries and minister to the orphans and widows in their homeland.

Our desire is not to be humanitarians. Our desire is to bring the kingdom of God here on earth. Our desire is that others will know Christ by this work.

Though the vision for the R.O.W. Project is overwhelming and the work immense, the Lord's hand is mightily moving. He has supernaturally provided in ways I could never dream of. His Word has been proven true time and time again.

There are times when it is hard. Self wants to reign again and proclaim that this is just too much time, effort, and cost. It is in these moments that God graces me with His presence. I am reminded of Him as one of the seven-year-old refugee girls puts her hand in mine and asks, "Can you please pray with me?"

There are no costs too high compared to knowing and experiencing the presence of Jesus Christ.

It is no longer the inner-city that I fear. Rather, it is the coffee shop that keeps me away from actually knowing firsthand the Lord's heartbeat.

—⊰⊱—

Beth's Story
Single Missionary to Jamaica

Ever since I was a little girl playing with my dollies, I always dreamed of the day I would be a wife and the mother of a few darling children. I was your typical girl raised in the era of the fifties and sixties when most mothers stayed at home to raise their children. My mother fit that mold to the letter.

My dream never changed throughout my life, but God clearly had something else in mind.

When I was in my late teens, I met a young man. His name was Bill. Neither one of us knew the Lord, but we thought we were on the right track. Very early in the relationship with Bill, I compromised my moral convictions in order to hold on to what I thought was love. It was not, but some of us must learn the hard way. We moved in together one year after we had met.

God, in His compassion, did not leave us wandering in the dark for long. Bill's mother told us of a new program on television that was all about God. We were eager to watch it because we really wanted to learn about Him. The program was called *100 Huntley Street*, and it was Canada's first Christian TV talk show, sharing the Good News of Jesus Christ. Both celebrities and ordinary folks expressed how Jesus Christ had changed their lives 100 percent! We loved the program and began watching it almost every day. I even skipped going to work sometimes in order to catch the program.

Well, as I began to watch this show on a regular basis, the message began to have quite an impact on my life. I figured that if

Jesus could change these people's lives, then He could probably change mine too. I knew my heart was not right before God, and so one day as I watched *100 Huntley Street*, the host, David Mainse, invited the TV audience to pray to ask Jesus Christ into their lives. I immediately bowed my head and prayed for God's forgiveness to take place in my life.

Over time the Holy Spirit's gentle-but-persistent conviction about Bill and me living together started a process within my heart. Within a year and a half our relationship ended. The Lord led me to return home to my parents to rekindle our family relationship. It was a wonderful two years that was a great blessing to us all.

During this time, while I was attending a very dynamic church, a Christian missionary organization, Youth With A Mission (YWAM), invited churches all over Ontario to come and participate with them in evangelism at the 1984 Summer Olympics held in Los Angeles. God clearly showed me that I was to go.

Little did I know, but He was planting a seed in my heart regarding missions. After I came back from an incredible time of evangelism in Los Angeles, I began reading biographies of missionaries like Jim and Elisabeth Elliot, Nate Saint, and Frank and Marie Drown. I couldn't seem to get enough of them. Working in an office in front of a computer didn't seem to have the same appeal anymore. I wanted to work with people—I wanted to be a missionary! Whatever that meant.

My young heart still wondered about marriage. "Lord, when will I find the man You have for me?" I queried. I had just recently chosen to lay down the intense feelings that I had for a young man at my church. I thought maybe he would be the one, but when I was really honest with God and my own heart, I knew the Lord wasn't really giving me true peace to pursue the relationship the way I wanted. We were always just to be friends. Once I released him to the Lord, with no strings attached, then, amazingly, I had peace. Hmm, maybe God had someone else in mind.

Within a little less than a year after the Summer Olympics, I was on my way to Tyler, Texas, to embark upon an exciting new adventure. I was going to learn how to be a missionary! I had applied to Youth With A Mission, Tyler, and my Discipleship Training School began in April 1985. The following year my training continued through the School of Evangelism. It was during this time that the Lord confirmed to my heart that He wanted me to become a teacher, something I had long forgotten about but had always wanted to be as a little girl. God's dream for my life was unfolding. It was beyond what I could have ever imagined.

God's wonderful leading and blessing were very precious, but at the same time, I was struggling with the Lord about THE DREAM— *Ah, remember, Lord, I REALLY want to get married and have a family. How come I'm not seeing any signs about that?*

My teacher training began through a type of apprenticeship at YWAM, Tyler. I loved all that I was learning and experiencing as I interacted with wise teachers and the precious children of the school. God's call to teach little children, laying a solid Christian foundation in their lives, was truly the fulfillment of His dream for me. I loved participating in His dream. It was and continues to be one of the most fulfilling experiences in my life.

The struggle regarding marriage continued for many years. I argued, kicked, and hollered for quite some time. However, I remember one day when I was taking a walk down a quiet Texas road. I was talking to the Lord, and I told Him that I didn't want Him *ever* to give in to my little pity parties about not having a husband. I had come to recognize the fact that His gifts to me are always good and just right for me. If marriage was not going to be His highest for me, then I trusted His judgment on the matter. In all honesty, God knew exactly what was best.

After teaching Grade One for several years in Tyler, Texas, the Lord led me to Jamaica, where I now teach and give leadership to a Christian school that is a ministry of YWAM, Jamaica. It is just another one of God's incredible miracles in my life.

The years have passed by and I am now in my fifties, yet I don't pine away for some dashing man to come sweep me off my feet the way I used to. There is great fulfillment in being single too. (Could you have told me this 20 years ago? Probably not.) I have learned to be at peace with the wonderful blessings God chooses for me. Contentment comes in trusting in His loving commitment to be all that I need Him to be in my life. There is, however, a dashing little guy who has swept me off my feet. He is my little Jamaican son, Colin, whom I am adopting. He is one of those GOOD gifts from my heavenly Father. Yes, the Lord had spoken to me many years ago, through a dream I had about this very thing. I would be a nursing mother to a child whose mother could not nurse him. God's dreams continue!

Gabi's Story

Single Missionary to China

At a very young age I was aware of God's hand on my life. By the age of eight, I had already heard Him calling me to the mission field of China. I reveled in being close to God when I was a child, but during my early teenage years I started to lose sight of Him, as many of us do. For a few years I became more interested in what I wanted than what God wanted. It got me into trouble, and I could feel in my soul that I was decaying into an extremely selfish version of me.

When I was 14 years old, the Columbine High School shooting happened. I was deeply affected by this tragedy because many of my friends at the church I attended were students at Columbine. I realized then that people as young as us could have their lives snuffed out in an instant. My heart turned toward Jesus that day in a way it hadn't in several years. In the midst of that tragedy I came to understand that a life lived in and for Him was the only life worth living. Shortly thereafter I went on a choir tour to Taiwan and Korea. This further sealed my desire to dedicate my life to God because it freshly reminded me of the call to the Chinese people He had placed in my heart when I was so young.

I won't say my life was all rainbows and butterflies after that. In fact, it was quite a grueling process over the next few years to break habits I had formed, habits that were all about me and not about Him. But through it all He held me firmly in His grip, and I fell more and more in love with this awesome and beautiful Savior every day. I was sold out for Jesus.

On my sixteenth birthday I made the decision to give Jesus control over the area of relationships in my life. It honestly didn't feel like a sacrifice to say, "Okay, God, You have full reign over my love story." In fact, it felt freeing to know He had it under control and I could just focus on Him and what He had called me to without the distraction of being worried I had to "find the right guy." Since then I've had one adventure after another, and I'm so grateful I wasn't distracted by the manhunt that the girls around me seemed to always be on.

I knew He held my heart and my life, so I drove on with determination into the things He had laid out before me. That's not to say that during high school and my years at university that I never felt interest in certain guys who seemed amazing to me. I'm still a girl, and there were moments when I felt that longing to have a companion to share life with. In those moments of longing I had to turn to my Jesus and say, "I've given this part of my life to You. Take it and do with it what You will." Even though it wasn't always easy, it was always amazingly good, because I could move on with confidence knowing that when it was the right time, He would bring that guy along.

During those years I focused more and more on what I knew lay ahead for me—China. I studied the language hard and went on two short-term trips over two summer breaks from college. It had been my dream for a long time to graduate from college and head straight to the field. For some reason I didn't think it was going to happen, but guess what...it did! Seven months after graduation I was living in China.

For a year I lived in a big city in Central China, and I realized something incredible...at that place and at that time it was vital for me to be single and to have my one true love be Jesus. Most of the friends God brought into my path during that year were unmarried young women who were students at the universities in the city where I lived. Because of my commitment to God in the area of relationships, an impact was made on these young women's lives as they observed my undistracted love of HIM.

I made a great discovery during this time as well—that pouring my life wholeheartedly into the lives of others in His name brought me overflowing joy as I realized that a young single girl, devoted to Him, could be used in big ways for His kingdom and His glory. I felt so humbled, so in awe, and so fulfilled each time I looked into the eyes of a Chinese girl and saw that the scales had fallen and she had seen Jesus.

There were also some deeply dark times during my year in China. Times when I had to cling to Him more than ever, and times when I really longed for my singleness to be over. I felt such a strong need for a teammate, a companion. During this time there was a moment when I thought that longing was going to be fulfilled, that there was going to be a man of God there at my side. I knew that if He was bringing this man into my life, it would be perfect, but in my heart I felt an ache as I thought that there could be someone else coming into the picture; that picture that had just been Jesus and myself for so long. As it turned out, the relationship didn't come to pass as I had thought, but it was okay because He was still there ever at my side...the One I had always turned to, the One who had never let me down, the One who loved me wholeheartedly and unconditionally—Jesus.

If there's one important thing I would want to tell my single sisters, it would be to use every opportunity to know Jesus better and to let Him be the One you turn to in every situation. These moments with Him as a single person are so precious, and singleness, I believe, is a time to be truly cherished as you draw near to

Him and He draws near to you. If and when that day comes when He decides to bring a prince into your story, you will be so grateful that you know Jesus as you do. I believe that human relationships only fully work when each individual involved is whole in Him. When both people in a marriage are secure in Christ FIRST, they are drawing on Him for their identity and their strength as they grow and develop as a couple.

I would also highly recommend pursuing with all your might those dreams and passions that God has placed inside of you during your single years. Pour yourself into serving others, whether that's at home, at school, at your job, or on the mission field. Service to others in Jesus' name with a genuine heart of love is one of the most fulfilling and joyous feelings, and this time of singleness is a time not to be missed as a servant of Christ.

Instead of waiting for my prince to come along before I pursue the passions God has placed in me, I want to pursue them now, running with all my might down the path laid out before me, trusting fully that when the right time comes, my path and the path of the man He has chosen for me will merge. And even if that never happens, I can rejoice, knowing that I'm in His hand and doing what He has asked me to do.

※

Jolene's Story

Single Foster Parent to Children in Need

I came to know Christ when I was a senior in high school. I had a religious upbringing but in reality it was just that...religious. I didn't understand what it meant to have Christ as the Master of my life. While in high school I began attending the youth group at a friend's church. The youth pastor taught in a way I had never heard before. Through his powerful teaching I learned what it meant to die to self and allow Christ to live in and through me. I knew that was what was missing, and I surrendered my life to Christ. Through college I continued to grow in my walk. However, it was when God took me out of my comfort zone and moved me to a new location alone that the growing process truly began.

I began my first job, teaching elementary school in a very low-income, broken town. Many of my students came from dysfunctional families with extreme problems. I cried many tears over these children because I felt so helpless to do anything for them. For years I had dreamed of being an adoptive parent, but I had no idea what God would truly ask of me in this area. I thought I would get married and my husband and I would adopt beautiful babies from around the world and have one big multicultural family. But God had something different in mind.

As I continued to teach elementary school and grieve over the lives of the students in my class, I yearned to provide them with a better home. My mother has always told me that there are so many children right here in America who need loving homes. I began to see how true that was. I decided to look into local adoptions. Honestly, I felt that it would lead to a dead end. I figured I would have to be married and of a certain age, just like the overseas adoptions had required. A friend of mine had adopted children from our hometown, so I began asking her about it. Two of her children had been adopted through the foster care system, and she told me that I was more than qualified to do the same.

So nearly three years ago I obtained the application to become a foster parent, but I never filled it out. I was working two jobs at the time and spending the weekends with my grandmother, who lived 80 miles away, so I could not commit to a child. Then, my grandmother passed away and I quit the second job. God challenged me to step out, just like Moses. It was time for me to do something practical to help these children. I felt called, single though I was, to become a foster parent to children in need.

I enrolled in the classes, finished the application, and received my foster care license in July. Nine days later I got a call, asking if

I would become a foster parent to a 12-year-old boy. It was a completely different scenario than I'd always envisioned, but I knew God was telling me to say yes!

I remember driving to pick him up for the first time. Fear and panic gripped my heart, and I wondered, *What in the world am I doing?* I wanted to turn around and run back to my peaceful, BORING life, but there was no turning back. God gave me strength to see it through. My foster son, Justin, is my pride and joy. I have cried many tears over how blessed I am to have him in my life. It feels as though he has always been in my life. Justin is now a bubbly, cheerful 13-year-old. He can be a complete gem one moment and make me crazy the next, but through it all I love him! He has brought so much joy to my life, and we are two peas in a pod. God knew what He was doing! There are days when I think about the peaceful home I once had, but I am quickly reminded how boring it was. There is no boredom now! Each day is a new adventure and I wake up each morning excited for what it will bring. Justin has taught me so much in the seven months he has lived with me. He has taught me how to love unconditionally, how to seek forgiveness when necessary (I am not a perfect parent), how to have an ENDLESS supply of patience, and how to have joy over the simple things in life. I will begin the adoption process for him in a few short months, and I look forward to calling him my son.

Caring for Justin has also dramatically altered my relationship with Christ. Sometimes when life is "typical," it is easy to rely less on God for our strength and more on ourselves. But, when you turn your life upside down, you quickly learn how inadequate you actually are. I could NEVER do this if God was not actually doing it through me. It is way too big for me to do. He shows me that each and every day, but He also provides the strength to live out each day in a way that changes Justin's life. Through this experience I have drawn closer to Christ as the Provider for ALL. He has to be the One to provide me with the energy, the patience, the love, the wisdom, and the peace to do this.

I am challenged every single moment of every single day. I have quickly learned what it means to truly die to self. Foster children are not your typical children. They have experienced more horror in their young lives than possibly ten adults do in a lifetime. They are broken, hurting children, and they desperately need the love and joy that every child should have. They enter your home with baggage, pain, and anger. This causes them to act out toward anyone and everyone at times. Through it all, Christ says, "These are My children. Please take care of them." I have had to give up many dreams that every parent has of raising lovely, angelic children who adore you. God has asked me to take care of "the least of these," and that is what I plan on doing for the rest of my life. This means that many children will enter my home—some will stay permanently (Justin, my current foster child, will more than likely become my adopted son), and others will be reunited with their families after I have had the privilege of ministering to them for just a season of their lives.

Through it all, God will use me to teach them about our life-altering God. It is my hope that every hug, every kind word, every prayer spoken over each child He brings into my life will eventually lead them to our Father.

Many people think what I am doing is quite odd, and some disagree with my decision to adopt because I am a single parent. However, as I draw nearer to Christ, all I can hear is Him saying, "This is My child. Please take care of him." I have to be more concerned with what my Lord says than what the world around me thinks. This may even mean dying to dreams I have once had, but for Christ, it is worth it all. My decision to become a foster/adoptive parent has shown me incredible things about the people around me. I must honestly say that I could not do this without the support and love of the people in my life. I am not raising this child alone. My church family, my biological family, and my friends all play an active role in raising Justin.

When I made it clear that I plan on adopting Justin once he becomes legally free for adoption, many people in my life were concerned. Many people worried that I am messing up my future by taking on a child. To them I am a successful, bright, 26-year-old with a fantastic future ahead of me. They worry that adopting Justin will take away my chances for marriage and "true" happiness. I do not buy into this whole logic. Christ never promised me marriage. He promised that if I am obedient to Him, He will bless me. Yes…I do desire marriage. However, above all things, I desire to please my Lord and be obedient to Him in ALL things. He has called me to take care of the "least of these," and in return He will take care of me. I have a fantastic future ahead of me, and I cannot wait to see what He has in store for me. I believe it will be beautifully unpredictable, and I will love every minute of it!

If I could encourage my single sisters with one thing, it would be "listen to Christ and act in obedience." It was when we were broken and lost that Christ reached out and set us free. He is calling us to do the same for these children. They are broken and lost and He wants us to reach out, wrap them in our arms, and set them free from the lives they are living. Do not be afraid. When we act in obedience, He provides us with everything we need to do His will. He will not call us into something big and then leave us to do it on our own. He wants to showcase His power through our lives, and He simply needs willing participants.

We are at the prime of our lives for changing the world through foster care and adoption. God's Word says, "The unmarried woman cares about the things of the Lord, that she may be holy both in body and in spirit" (1 Corinthians 7:34). As single women we have been given a great gift! We have nothing holding us back from changing the world for Christ! I am an ordinary girl who is allowing the Lord to do extraordinary things through me, and every other single girl out there has the same potential. Take that step of faith and watch the blessings flow!

If you are interested, contact your local Child and Family Services Division. The phone number is found in the government section of your local phone book. Every state has different requirements, but they can lead you in the right direction. The Lord is pleading for us to take care of His children—and you may be the one to answer that call!

Getting Started Changing the World
Resources and Opportunities

As Christ demonstrated, love is not a feeling—it is something you do.
He then made it simple for us to understand when He said that pure
and undefiled religion is to take care of the widow and the orphan.
DANITA ESTRELLA, SINGLE MISSIONARY TO HAITI

Just yesterday I was speaking on a radio program about exchanging your own selfish pursuits for a poured-out life of service in Christ's kingdom. A single woman called in to the show and said, "My heart is so stirred by what you are saying. I want desperately to give my life to something meaningful for the kingdom of God, but I have no idea where to start."

I have heard this statement from countless young women. Though the world is literally flooded with people who are starving, exploited, impoverished, and destitute, America often shelters us from that reality. We live in a palace of luxury while countless people lay sick, enslaved, and dying just outside the walls of our castle. And if we never venture outside our walls of comfort, we'll never know how we can help meet the overwhelming needs of our day. God's Word says, "To whom much is given, from him much will be required" (Luke 12:48). We are the ones to whom much has been given. Modern advertising and pop culture constantly tries to imply that we aren't "there yet"—that we need to keep acquiring more and more material wealth. As a result, most of us don't realize how much we truly have in comparison to the rest of the world. Even those of us who are not considered wealthy by America's standard are among the wealthiest people who have ever existed in all of history.

A lot of us subconsciously say, "If I ever saw a person in need of food or clothing, of course I would help them!" But for those of us who live in middle-class suburban America, those opportunities don't come along very often. And it's all too easy to simply forget about the need that is out there because we are too preoccupied living our own lives and taking care of our own needs.

If you have struggled with discontentment in your singleness, one of the best solutions outside of cultivating daily intimacy with Jesus Christ is to forget about yourself and focus instead on serving and loving people in need. It's somewhat counterintuitive, but it works! Putting others' needs above your own doesn't lead to disappointment and misery, but to unmatched joy and fulfillment. My assistant, Annie, just returned from a week ministering to orphans in Haiti. She stayed in the middle of a crowded, dirty, poverty-stricken city full of heartache, noise, and violence. It was swelteringly hot. She hardly had any sleep. She spent six hours riding in a stuffy non-air-conditioned bus, transporting 20 children from one orphanage to another on rough, bumpy, crowded roads with virtually nonexistent traffic signals. There was no entertainment or distraction from the sick, starving, and sad children who clamored for her attention day in and day out. It doesn't sound like much of a vacation. But Annie had the time of her life. She came back bursting with joy and excitement. She never felt so alive or fulfilled as when she was living among the least and giving her all to them.

As Annie showed her photos and described her love for these children, her face glowed with a radiance that reminded me of a young woman who had just become engaged. How can living in sweltering heat, crowded cities, and uncomfortable conditions bring the same kind of thrill that a freshly budding love story does? It's just the way God's pattern works. When we go where He is and do what He does, we experience joy we never knew was possible. The world says that selfishness is the way to get the fulfillment we crave. But in God's economy, *selflessness* is what leads to real joy.

If you feel a stirring in your heart to live a more others-focused life, this chapter is meant to help give you practical ideas for how to begin. By no means is this an exhaustive list of the opportunities that are out there. It is very possible that God will open up something for you that's completely different from what I've mentioned here. For example, I recently met a young woman who feels called to reach the deaf around the world with the message of the Gospel. She has spent the last several years learning sign language and taking every opportunity she can find to travel and interact with deaf people in impoverished countries. That struck me as such a unique and much-needed ministry!

It's so important that we allow God to guide and direct our steps when it comes to these decisions. He knows the plans He has for us, and if we are diligent to seek Him, He will make our path clear. However, just because we don't have clarity on all of the details shouldn't stop us from moving forward. Often, God will only give us a small ray of light to follow, keeping all the "hows" and "whens" hidden until we take that first step of obedience. Jackie Pullinger knew only that she was supposed to "go" and reach poor people with the hope of Christ. She boarded a ship that was sailing around the world and prayed about where God would have her get off. Gladys Aylward knew only that God wanted her in China, so with virtually no money or contacts she boarded a train and allowed God to handle the details. Lydia Prince only felt a draw to Jerusalem. She had no idea how God would choose to use her there, but she went anyway. In every case God performed miracle after miracle to direct these courageous women's paths. When we step out in obedience to Him, He will always go with us!

As you read through the practical ideas offered in this chapter, I would encourage you to pray that God's Spirit would be your guide. Ask Him to stir your heart toward a specific cause. Ask Him to clarify how He might want to use your life to build His kingdom. And ask Him to give you courage to take the first step forward.

Ways to Help Orphans

There are 143 million orphans in the world today.[1] They are hungry, sick, scared, and alone. They ache for love, for a family, for an advocate. Their world is harsh and cruel. Countless millions live on the streets. They are treated as the scum of society. They must scavenge through dumps to find food. They inhale chemical solvents to ease their hunger pains. In many countries, even stray dogs get more respect than these precious little ones. They hide in cemeteries or old buildings to escape being shot and killed by corrupt men, and to avoid being kidnapped and forced into sex slavery. Many do not live past their sixteenth birthday. They perish in agony from hunger, sickness, glue addiction, and sexually transmitted disease.

The AIDS crisis is one of the largest disasters in world history. Children are the greatest victims. Fifteen million have already been orphaned in Africa because of AIDS.[2] But the staggering fact is that within the next two years, that number is predicted to jump to 40 million. The children orphaned by AIDS are often infected with HIV themselves, facing a bleak future of starvation, sickness, and death.

In Northern Uganda, an unfathomable crisis has been unfolding for the past several years. The so-called Lord's Rebel Army has kidnapped thousands of children, raping them, killing their parents, and forcing them to kill their family members or be killed themselves. Thousands and thousands of children have been orphaned, displaced, and abused beyond comprehension because of this terrible atrocity. And yet we hear only snippets of this crisis from time to time in American news. Thousands of children from the villages of Uganda must walk miles and miles each night to take refuge in the nearest town, sleeping in old buildings and on the street in order to escape abduction from the LRA.

In Haiti, Cambodia, Vietnam, and many other countries, staggering numbers of orphan girls are being kidnapped and forced into slave prostitution—some as young as five years old. One documentary I watched interviewed a 24-year-old Cambodian woman who had been forced into sex slavery from the age of 13. She was required to sleep with 15 men a day, and she was beaten or shocked with electricity whenever she tried to refuse. Now, at 24, she is dying from AIDS. Her greatest fear, she confesses, is that when she dies, no one will come to her burial.

This young woman could be any one of us. How can we possibly sit by passively when such injustice toward children is taking place all over the world?

Rees Howells, an early nineteenth-century missionary and prayer warrior, once felt God challenge him to become a "father to the fatherless." There was a family of orphan children in Rees' town, and God challenge him to take them as his own. "I thought You were the Father to the fatherless, God," Rees countered in protest. "Yes," God replied. "But you are part of my Body. You are My hands and feet. For Me to truly be a Father to the fatherless, I must be one through you."[3]

God wants us to be fathers and mothers to the orphans of the world. It's a sacred call upon every one of our lives—not a special call—as James 1:27 clearly states.

It can be overwhelming to think about how to rescue the 143 million orphans of the world. And it certainly is not easy to reach them. In fact, it's far easier to be a corrupt child exploiter than an advocate for the orphan. I recently watched a documentary by ABC News called *How to Buy a Child Slave in 10 Hours*. A news reporter, disguised as an American traveler, flew from New York City to Port-au-Prince, Haiti, and within ten hours had brokered a deal to purchase a ten-year-old girl for $150. On the other hand, I know of many families who have been trying to adopt an orphan from that same country for more than two years. They have spent thousands of dollars and endured agonizing delays in order to finally rescue just *one* child. It's an infuriating reality that a corrupt child abuser can obtain an orphan for $150 in less than 10 hours, while an orphan advocate must spend tens of thousands of dollars and be forced to hack through mountains of red tape and governmental policy in order to bring a needy child home.

We must remember that when Jesus rescued us, it was not easy or quick. It required far more discomfort and pain than we could possibly imagine. And when we become His hands and feet to these little ones around the world, we should not expect an easy road either.

Even in America, orphans exist. They are known as foster care children. It is politically incorrect to call them "orphans" nowadays, so often the church overlooks them as not truly being in need of assistance. But foster care children are often as needy as abandoned street children around the world. The lucky ones are placed into loving Christian homes, but the majority of them are trapped in chaotic, unhealthy, abusive living environments, overlooked, rejected, and unloved. They are victims of a dysfunctional system that is heavy on policies but severely lacking in personal advocacy. When foster care kids are of age, many are simply kicked out of the system and left to fend for themselves. I've heard people try to defend the foster care system in America, or downplay the fact that these children should truly be considered orphans worthy of our assistance, but the startling fact that more than 70 percent of prisoners in America are former foster kids speaks volumes about the urgent need for reform.[4]

Ask God to show you where to start. Sometimes, He asks us to begin with one. When Eric and I first began to feel the call of God to reach the orphans of the world, the idea was daunting. We didn't know where to begin. And then we heard about a two-month-old orphan girl from South Korea with no fingers. And we knew this was the one God wanted us to start with. (Today, this little girl is our daughter, Harper Grace Ludy.)

My assistant, Annie, has had a passion for orphans for many years. Yet she hasn't known exactly what group of orphans to focus on. One of her desires was to use her photography skills to minister to orphans in some way. So she began to pray that God would open a door for that to happen, and she began to be on the lookout for those opportunities. Seemingly out of nowhere, she found out about an orphanage in Haiti that needed a photographer to take pictures of children waiting to be adopted. And she knew it was the door she had been praying for.

When you allow God to place orphans on your radar screen and ask Him to open doors for you to reach them, you'll be amazed at the doors that open.

Below are a few steps to consider taking.

Visit Orphan Websites

Go online to increase your awareness of the need and opportunities with orphans around the world. Some of my favorites are:

- www.worldorphans.org
- www.cryoftheorphan.org
- www.hopefororphans.com
- www.abandoned-orphaned.org
- www.helporphans.org

Help Meet Orphans' Needs

Give an orphanage a washing machine, crib, package of diapers, etc. At www.helporphans.org, you can click on the "Gift from the Heart" section and designate a financial gift to be used for an item of your choice to be given to an orphanage in the country of your choice. You can also organize a drive to collect shoes or other supplies for orphans around the world. Visit www.shoesfororphansouls.org or www.gainusa.org and click on "Projects." At www.worldorphans.org you can learn how a gift of a few thousand dollars can cover building costs of a new orphanage in one of dozens of countries. Consider helping raise this money through your small group or church.

A couple of specific orphan ministries that have stood out to

Eric and me are Danita's Children (an orphan ministry in Haiti) and Acres of Hope (an orphan ministry in Liberia). As Karris mentioned earlier, Danita's Children was started by a single woman who felt called to go to Haiti with very little money and no real missionary experience. The story of how God led her to begin a ministry to orphans that now houses 75 orphans and reaches more than 500 children every week with food, clothing, and education is truly remarkable. For more details about Danita's ministry and how you might be able to help, visit www.danitaschildren.org.

Acres of Hope was started by a mother of 16 children, most of whom are adopted, with missing limbs or other special medical needs. She developed a heart for Liberia, one of the most devastated and impoverished countries in the world, and the orphanage she built has currently helped more than 300 orphans find the food, shelter, medicine, and love they desperately needed. Her book, *Acres of Hope*, is a powerful story about how one obedient woman is changing the world for Christ. Visit www.acresofhope.org to learn more about this ministry and how you might be able to help.

Attend the Annual Orphan Summit (sponsored by Focus on the Family, Family Life, and Shaohannah's Hope)

This is an annual three-day conference in which orphan advocates gather together to learn more about orphan needs around the world, connect with others in orphan-ministry, and gain God's heart for the fatherless. Eric and I have attended this event numerous times and have always been deeply impacted and practically assisted in our efforts to stand for orphans. For more information about this event, visit www.cryoftheorphan.org.

Pray for Orphans

Here is a practical prayer suggestion from Family Life Today's orphan ministry:

> There are countless numbers of "waiting children" around the world and in our own country; kids who are up for

adoption, hoping and praying for a forever-family. Pray for waiting kids whenever you are "waiting." Go online to find a waiting child listing. A few of these listings include: www.adoptuskids.org; www.rainbowkids.com; www.precious.org. Print out a picture and description of a waiting child and tape it to your dashboard. Every time you find yourself waiting—in traffic, at a stoplight, in the drive-thru—pray for this child. Plead with the Father on their behalf. Organize an evening prayer vigil on behalf of the orphan and waiting child. Invite other churches to join you as well. You can pray for children all over the world or you can ask your local foster care office for pictures and names of waiting children in your city to pray for. (You can also get these online.)

You can also become a spokesperson for waiting kids. Keep a picture of a waiting child in your wallet or purse. When you are visiting with other believers, pull it out and ask if they, or someone else they know, would consider giving this child a home. Often, the idea of adopting a waiting child seems impossible from a distance, but when people are able to take an up close look at a specific child, their entire perspective changes.[5]

Visit an Orphanage

You can go on a construction trip, a medical trip, or just a simple outreach trip to interact with these precious children and show them the love of Christ. One orphanage director I spoke with recently said that just having someone spend individual time with an orphanage child can make a huge impact—because so often these kids cannot receive one-on-one attention. Some ministries that organize frequent trips to orphanages around the world are:

- www.gainusa.org
- www.helporphans.org
- www.hopechest.org

Sponsor an Orphan

This includes both monthly financial support and a ministry of ongoing encouragement though letter writing. Visit www.hopechest.org, www.visiontrust.org, or www.worldhelp.org to learn more. Child sponsorship can make the difference between health or sickness, education or poverty, hope or despair, and usually requires such a small sacrifice on our part.

Consider Long-term Orphan-Work Positions

It's easy to assume that there are lots of other people out there working to solve the orphan crisis. But with 143 million orphans in the world, the need is not going to disappear anytime soon. In many impoverished countries, you can simply walk down the street and observe hundreds of street children begging for food, scouring through trash, and sleeping in gutters or on dumps. Most orphanages I've encountered started with one simple man, woman, or couple who moved to a developing nation and made themselves available to orphans. Without fail, orphans flocked to them as a refuge and safe haven—and that's how the orphanage was launched. It didn't require a lot of money, strategy, or expertise. It simply required availability and a mighty faith in God.

If God is stirring your heart to pour out your life for orphans on a more permanent basis, I would encourage you to follow His lead! Visit orphanages around the world and ask Him to show you where and how to begin. Typically, orphanages in developing nations are desperately needing full-time staff to care for the children, administrate finances, teach, and disciple. Just this week I've received two emails from orphan directors in Haiti, urgently needing full-time positions by people who have either nursing or administration skills. These are just two of the countless opportunities that are out there. Don't worry about the fact that you do not know the language or that you lack experience. Allow God to expand your vision and fill your heart with courage to step out in faith and confidence that He will direct your steps!

Danita Estrella (mentioned earlier) was a single American woman in a successful career when she felt God's call to pour out her life for the orphan and widow. Without much missionary training or background, she wasn't sure that God could really use her on the mission field. But in obedience, she moved to Haiti and asked God to direct her steps. Here is how she described those first few months:

> When I first arrived in Haiti, I was not sure where God was leading me. I would walk the streets with sadness and weep before God as I saw hungry homeless children just trying to survive. But His purpose for me was still not clear. What difference could I possibly make? Besides, I had no prior missions experience. I was single. I did not know the language. And I had very little income. But if God was for me, who could be against me?[6]

Today, Danita's orphanage is home to 75 children, and she reaches many hundreds more each week through her school, church, and feeding program. She is living proof of what God can do through a fully yielded life.

Help Facilitate Adoption

Psalm 68:5 says God is "a father of the fatherless," and He "sets the solitary in families" (Psalm 68:6). Isaiah says that those who "bring to your house the poor who are cast out" will be blessed by God (Isaiah 58:7). Adoption is very close to God's heart. In fact, adoption is an amazing picture of the Gospel. When we receive Christ, we are adopted into the family of God, and receive the amazing, unmatched privilege of being His sons and daughters for eternity. A "forever family" is the number one desire of every orphan child. One orphan worker told me recently of a six-year-old girl in Guatemala who cries herself to sleep every night because she longs so desperately for a family. Millions of children echo her cries.

In spite of the desperate need for families for the orphans of the world, adoption is not as popular or widespread as might be expected. Only 17,000 international adoptions take place in the U.S. each year. That's not many considering the millions and millions of babies and children desperately needing families.[7]

Having personally walked through two adoption processes, I understand why the adoption numbers are so low. The process, in most cases, is extremely expensive and very intimidating. Families feel unable to afford it and are often overwhelmed by the endless piles of paperwork, government forms, and invasive home studies from social workers. As I said earlier, it's far easier and cheaper to obtain an orphan child for corrupt purposes than to rescue one for the kingdom of God.

But there is a lot that you can do to help make adoption more viable for Christian families. Churches around this country are beginning to awaken to the idea of launching ministry expressly dedicated to orphans and waiting children, providing funding, support, prayer, and practical help to families seeking to adopt. You can become the catalyst in your church for launching an orphan/adoption ministry. To learn how, visit www.shaohannahshope.org or www.hopefororphans.com.

You can also give financially to two organizations that provide grant money to families seeking to adopt. From personal experience, I can say that both of these organizations were truly amazing and critical in helping us afford our daughter's adoption from Korea. To find out more, visit www.lifesongfororphans.org and www.shao hannahshope.org.

More Ways to Support Adoption

Become a licensed social worker and provide home study services through a local Christian adoption agency. Most Christian families dread the idea of walking through the home study process, in which a social worker meets with you to ask you personal questions about your marriage, lifestyle, and how you raise your kids. Just knowing that they will have the opportunity to work with a like-minded Christian social worker provides a huge amount of relief, and it often makes the difference between a family saying yes or no to adoption.

If you know a family thinking about adoption, encourage them and offer practical support. A great resource is the booklet *Welcome Home: Eight Steps to Adoption,* available through Family Life Today (www. store.familylife.com). There is also a great book called *Successful Adoption: A Guide for Christian Families,* which is filled with essential information and inspiring adoption stories. If it seems appropriate, purchase these resources and give them to Christian families you know who are contemplating adoption. Sometimes just having someone give them a little encouraging push in the right direction is all it takes.

If you know of someone who is adopting, offer to throw a shower for them. The adoption process is just as exciting, emotional, and lifelong as pregnancy and childbirth, but often adoptive parents are not treated with the same support or enthusiasm from friends and family. By throwing the adoptive family a shower, you can help them celebrate the miracle of adopting a child into their home, just as if they were bringing a child into their home by birth. You can also organize meals to be taken to an adoptive family upon the arrival of their child. When Harper came home from Korea, one of our neighbors organized several families from the neighborhood to bring meals to us for the first week. It was so helpful and appreciated— especially since Eric and I were getting very little sleep and didn't have time or energy to cook!

Another great way to support adoption is to connect with a local crisis pregnancy center (also called pregnancy resource centers). You can volunteer to become a counselor for women facing unwanted pregnancies or help the pregnancy ministry in many other practical ways. It is a sad reality that Planned Parenthood and other proabortion organizations receive millions of dollars of funding from the government and other sources, while pro-adoption ministries often struggle to make ends meet. You can offer to help your local pregnancy center with their fund-raising efforts and even become trained as a grant writer to propose and submit grants to various organizations that may potentially offer financial support. Visit www.care-net.org for a list of pregnancy centers around the country.

What About Adopting as a Single Woman?

If God lays adoption on your heart, it's not out of the question for you to prayerfully consider providing foster care or even adopting a child yourself, especially if you are an older single in your late twenties, thirties, or beyond; are at least somewhat financially established; and have a great Christian support system around you. Of course, this decision is one of the biggest you will ever make in your life, and it should not be made haphazardly. If God has placed this desire in your heart, commit the decision to faithful, diligent prayer (and consider recruiting a trusted godly teammate to pray along with you) until you have the absolute peace and certainty that this is what He is leading you to do. If you know other single adoptive families, talk to them about their experiences.

If you adopt through the United States foster care system, there is no cost to you. And if you adopt overseas, there are many grants and tax benefits that might help fund the expense. Eric and I are friends with a single man in his thirties who recently adopted two brothers with special needs. It is beautiful to see how he has become a loving and godly father to these boys, who would have grown up in the "system" without him.

Rita Springer, a Christian worship leader, writes in *Successful Adoption* about how God led her, as a single woman, to become a mother to a little boy in need.

> I was thirty-seven years old, and my whole life I had dreamed of being a soccer mom. But here I was, still single. I was faithfully praying and waiting on the Lord, I even had dreams about my husband. I had pictured adopting a child someday, but I never pictured myself doing it alone. I thought my husband and I would adopt a child from Africa together. Then I visited a Romanian hospital and saw all these babies

just dying right there in their cribs, and I felt the Lord start talking to me about adoption. I didn't know what to do. I really wasn't sure I was prepared to be a single mom. I had doubts and fears. I was raised in a loving, Christian home, but I also knew what it was like to lose parental figures at a young age. I was nine when my dad died of cancer, and my mother died nine years after that. I knew what it was like not to have a dad, and I didn't feel it would be fair to raise a child without one. That's when God told me, "Your dad died when you were nine, and I did a good job fathering you. You and I have done all these things together. Let's go raise a warrior together." Wow! I knew then that I was being called to go down that road and adopt.[8]

Only a few months later, though a miraculous series of events, Rita was mother to a newborn little boy whose birth parents were from Africa. Though she adopted in the U.S., God answered her desire to adopt a child from Africa. Her dream is to raise her son as a warrior for God's kingdom, and that someday he will return to Zimbabwe to spread the Gospel.

If you are seriously considering adoption for yourself, a great starting place would be getting the two resources I mentioned earlier: *Welcome Home: Eight Steps to Adoption* and the book *Successful Adoption: A Guide for Christian Families*.

Reach Out to Foster Care Children

More than 20,000 teens a year "age out" of the U.S. foster care system with no place to call home.[9] Call your local foster care office and let them know you have the desire to be a support for a child who is aging out of foster care. I recently encountered a nineteen-year-old Christian single young woman who has launched a support system for teens who have aged out of the foster care system. She helps them gain practical skills, emotional support, and day-to-day assistance to help them make a strong start in their new life and overcome many of the intense challenges they face. We are in need of many, many more advocates for these young people across our country.

Other Ways to Reach Foster Care Children

Become a court appointed special advocate. These are people who volunteer their time to get to know a child in foster care and speak to the court on their behalf. You can find out more by visiting www .nationalcasa.org.

Care packages for crisis situations. Because of drugs, alcohol, violence, and abuse, foster children are sometimes pulled out of their homes with no warning, even in the middle of the night. They are often thrust into a new environment without their familiar toys, blankets, clothes, or basic necessities. Volunteer to make a care package for children who are taken out of crisis situations—and include items such as stuffed animals, blankets, a toothbrush and toothpaste. It can be a simple way to bring comfort and peace in an emotionally turbulent moment.

Support local foster care families. Volunteer to babysit, help with housework, cook a meal for them once a week, etc. Commit to praying for these courageous families and offer them words of encouragement. Offer to provide "respite care," meaning temporary foster care, to give the long-term foster families a reprieve. You can connect with foster care families through your local foster care agency. Just do a quick search online, and you'll find a list of options.

Get creative. Here's one example: A couple of years ago, a 17-year-old Florida girl named Lindsay began praying about an outreach—some sort of ministry she could participate in—some way to utilize her unique gifts for God's glory. Lindsay got the idea to launch a ministry called Taylor's Closet. It allows girls in foster care to come into a storelike environment and "shop" for whatever clothes they like, completely free of charge. The idea was just to put a smile on their face for a moment and let them know they weren't alone.

Since then God has blessed this ministry in some huge and wonderful ways. In December 2006, Taylor's Closet opened its first permanent "store" for foster girls—a boutique filled with new or barely used designer clothes that the girls can take home for free. Taylor's Closet receives clothing donations from all over the world and gives girls in foster care a place to come where they feel loved in a truly practical way. Visit ww.taylorscloset.org to get the full story and perhaps be inspired toward *your own* unique idea for reaching out to these precious foster care kids.

Here are a few more examples:

In Colorado, two Christian men recently started something called Project 127 (as in James 1:27) with the goal to help get all of the state's 800 "waiting kids" into adoptive Christian families. They hold seminars in churches all over the region, linking prospective parents with waiting children, helping facilitate the adoption process, and providing support, encouragement, and practical help for those who adopt.

Another local ministry, Portraits of Hope, takes beautiful portrait-style photography of waiting children and displays them in church lobbies and at Christian seminars, so that potential families can see the children up close and catch a vision for the idea of adopting them.

Ways to Help the Poor

About 25,000 people die every day from hunger or hunger-related causes, according to the United Nations. That's one person every three and a half seconds. At www.poverty.com you can see a world map that details where hunger deaths are happening currently around the world, and even see names and photos of people who have died in the past hour from poverty and starvation (don't worry, it's not morbid—the photos shown are from when they were alive). It is truly heartbreaking, and I find I have a hard time looking at this website for too long because of the sick knot that forms in my stomach as I see these precious faces of lives that have wasted away from poverty.

Amy Carmichael wrote,

> Far off, sorrowful things are perhaps endurable. It is always possible to disbelieve them.

John Donne said,

> Ignorance is not only the drowsiness, the silliness, but the wickedness of the soul. The cruelest man alive could not sit at his feast unless he sat blindfolded.

I fear that all too many of us, myself included, have spent years sitting blindfolded at our own feasts, enjoying the pleasures and comforts of plenty while countless lives around the world waste away from hunger and poverty. Let us no longer endure sorrowful things because they are so far away and so hard to believe. As God's set-apart young women, we are called to *open our eyes* to the need around the world—and not only to open our eyes, but to make ourselves available to be eyes to the blind, feet to the lame, and justice for the poor (see Job 29).

When Annie returned from Haiti, she told us about children with bloated bellies and discolored hair from lack of nutrition. The average Haitian child eats a meal once every three days. Many eat dirt mixed with flour and water to fill the ache in their bellies. Haiti has the highest infant mortality rate in the Western Hemisphere. While Annie was there, 30 parents came to the orphanage to relinquish their children for adoption in order to preserve their lives. The parents simply could not feed their children, so they were forced to give them up. It broke Annie's heart to take photographs of parents who were forcing their kids to smile for the camera in the hope that some American family would take an interest in them and give them a chance to survive.

I recently watched a documentary about impoverished children in Kenya called Glue Boys. Thousands of children sleep on the street, scavenge trash bins for scraps of food, and inhale chemical solvents to ease their hunger pains. Many of these kids die in their teen years or sooner, if not from starvation and disease, then from poisoning their body with glue sniffing.

Last year, I read about the thousands of street children in South America who live on garbage dumps and eat buzzards and dead dogs to survive. Tears of horror and despair ran down my face because I felt helpless to rescue them.

But with God, we are far from helpless! His heart is close to poor people of the earth. And He will be with us if we stand for them. Isaiah says:

> Is this not the fast that I have chosen: To loose the bonds of wickedness, to undo the heavy burdens, to let the oppressed go free, and that you break every yoke? Is it not to share your bread with the hungry, and that you bring to your house the poor who are cast out; when you see the naked, that you cover him, and not hide yourself from your own flesh? (Isaiah 58:6-7).

This is God's call upon each of us who proclaims to know Him. If we want to walk with Him, we cannot ignore the cries of the poor.

Below are some practical ways to get started being His hands and feet to them.

Visit Websites

Go online to help expand your awareness of poverty around the world. Some of my favorites are:

- www.poverty.com
- www.worldhelp.com
- www.worldhope.com
- www.glueboys.com

Listen to Jackie Pullinger's Messages on the Poor

These can be found at www.sermonindex.net. If you listen with your heart and allow God's Spirit to speak to you, your life will never be the same. Two of my favorites are "Lord, Give Me Your Heart" and "God Uses the Foolish Things."

Give

When you consider that the amount of money most of us spend at Starbucks each month can feed a starving child for that same amount of time, it makes you stop and reevaluate where your money is going. Just as we will be accountable to God for every idle word we speak (Matthew 12:36), we will be accountable for every careless dime we spend. There is a global food crisis going on around the world. Emergency help is needed or countless more will die. According to Compassion International, $39 will sustain an entire family for a month, and $79 will sustain two families. Consider giving sacrificially to the poor of the world. Are there comforts you can go without in order to meet this urgent need? Sponsor a child, sponsor a family, support organizations that are meeting their needs. There are loads of ministries to the poor in desperate need of funding. Visit these websites to learn more:

- www.compassion.com
- www.poverty.com
- www.worldhelp.org
- www.worldhope.com

Go Serve the Poor Around the World

If you listen to Jackie Pullinger's message "Lord, Give Me Your Heart," you will be challenged to the core with the call to *go*—to get out of your comfort zone and go to the poorest and neediest people on earth. The poor of the world do not just need Americans to throw money at them—they also need us to go to them, to live among them, to love them, serve them, give to them, and meet their practical and spiritual needs.

Jackie talked about going to live in the Walled City of Hong Kong, China, among the most impoverished and destitute people in the world. It took her nearly 20 years to gain their trust. They had seen Americans and Europeans come and go—usually getting off their air-conditioned airplanes, wearing designer clothes, staying in fancy hotels, and coming to the Walled City for a few hours a day to play their guitar and sing worship songs and hand out tracts. After a week they would leave and fly back to their comfortable lives back home. And the people of the Walled City said to Jackie, "They leave, but we are still here. Those Americans came only to ease their own conscience. They did not meet any of our needs. They still have everything and we have nothing. What impact do they expect to make?" Jackie was able to reach their souls with the message of Christ because she didn't place herself above them. She lived in the Walled City with them. She shared her house, her food, even her own bedroom with those in need.

To truly reach the poor with the hope of the Gospel, we have to be willing to live among them and sacrifice for them, just as Jesus did for us. Are we willing to give up our lives for them?

Not everyone is called to spend 20 years living in the Walled City, but we are certainly called to more than a short-term feel-good mission trip once every two years. Pray about where God wants you to go to reach the poor, whether it is for a season or for the rest of your life. Read inspiring stories of women who answered God's called to *go* such as: Lottie Moon, Mary Slessor, Lydia Prince, Jackie Pullinger, Gladys Aylward, and Amy Carmichael.

Serve the Poor in America

While the poor in America aren't usually as destitute as the poor around the world, there are still countless families in this country who are struggling with the basics of daily life, such as food, shelter, and clothing. Visit your local rescue mission or homeless shelter to learn about opportunities in your area. You can also get involved with inner-city churches in your area to link with poor families in need of assistance. Some other great resources are www.salvation armyusa.org and www.samaritanpurse.org.

Ways to Help Rescue Slaves

I loved the movie *Amazing Grace* about the life of William

Wilberforce—a man who labored tirelessly to end the slave trade in the late 1700s. His dream was finally realized in 1807 when the Slave Trade Act was passed, and England's slave trade was abolished. I left the movie wishing I had such a noble cause to give my life to. And then I learned that human slavery still exists today. In fact, it is even higher than in the days of William Wilberforce—higher than it has ever been throughout all of world history, in fact.

There are 27 million slaves in the world today, and millions more exploited children. Countless men, women, and children are exploited for sex slavery or forced labor. Approximately 80 percent are women, and at least 50 percent are children.

It is estimated that there are 246 million exploited children between 5 and 17 involved in debt bondage, forced recruitment for armed conflict, prostitution, pornography, the illegal drug trade, the illegal arms trade, and other illicit activities around the world.

Girls trapped in sex slavery are lured by phony promises of work, marriage, educational advances, or a better life—jobs that traffickers turn into the nightmare of prostitution without exit. Women and girls, some as young as seven, are tortured, beaten, and repeatedly raped into submission. Entrapment is perpetuated by torture, beatings, starvation, death threats to victims or loved ones, and confiscation of travel/identification documents.

Here is what the Salvation Army says about the current slavery crisis:

> Each year traffickers supply millions of human beings for labor exploitation in settings such as brick kilns, sweatshops, chicken farms, cocoa plantations, mines, fisheries, rock quarries, or for compulsory participation in public works or military service, as well as a variety of other settings. Countless others, predominately women and female children, but also boys, are trafficked into the commercial sex industry where they are used in forms of commercial sexual exploitation like prostitution, pornography, and nude dancing. Some are sold as "brides." Trafficking in persons

is frequently referred to as modern-day slavery. Slavery is an apt analogy that shocks and challenges us. Americans in particular are moved by this comparison. To us, slavery is a sordid, indelible stain on our national heritage, but nevertheless it is an evil most believe we conquered and relegated to the history books. However, news media accounts, on-the-ground intelligence from nongovernmental organizations, and reports from agencies the U.S. Department of State and the United Nations Office on Drugs and Crime, create a different picture. They reveal a hideous yet inescapable truth: slavery is alive.[10]

One girl I read about was kidnapped by sex traffickers in Brazil when she was nine years old. She was held at a brothel in a remote part of the Amazon, forced to be a prostitute and obey the whims of corrupt businessmen and tourists. When she tried to escape, she was caught and tied to the back of a truck by her arms and drug through back alleys and dirt roads until she nearly died. I read about other girls, as young as five years old, whose virginity was "auctioned" away to the highest bidder. By the time these girls reach their teen years, they are wasting away from sexual disease and have lost their value to the sex industry. Most are turned out onto the streets to die.

I recently saw a documentary in which an undercover reporter posed as a sex tourist in Cambodia and encountered a back alley brothel in which dozens of six-, seven-, and eight-year-old girls were available for sex for the price of $30.

Even in the U.S. human trafficking is rampant. The State Department estimates that 75,000 women and children are illegally brought into the U.S. annually for forced prostitution and other forms of slave labor. They estimate that 50 percent of them are trafficked for sexual exploitation.[11]

The more you learn about this issue, the less you can keep quiet. Slaves around the world are in desperate need of advocates. With the help of God, we can make an eternal impact in their lives and fulfill the call of Isaiah 58 to let the oppressed go free. Below are some ways to begin.

Visit Websites

Go online to become aware of the human trafficking issue around the world:

- www.projectrescue.com
- www.ijm.org
- www.salvationarmyusa.org
  (click on "Fight Human Trafficking")
- www.countcampaign.org

Watch the Following Videos/Documentaries About Human Slavery:

- *Sex Slavery in Cambodia*
  www.ijm.org/video/viewcategory
- *A Child Prostitute's Story*
  www.youtube.com/watch?v=IEclmPZZKh8&feature=related
- *How to Buy a Child Slave in 10 Hours*
  abcnews.go.com/search?searchtext=Child%20Slavery%20in%20Haiti&type=

Read the Following Books on Human Slavery:

- *This Immoral Trade*
- *A Crime So Monstrous*

Get Connected with Anti-Trafficking Ministries

To learn about ways you can help, go to:

- www.projectrescue.com
- www.ijm.com

- www.ucountcampaign.org
- www.salvationarmyusa.org

Other People in Need of Your Help
The Imprisoned

> *I was in prison, and you came to me.*
> (MATTHEW 25:36)

Voice of the Martyrs, a ministry that reaches persecuted Christians around the world, says this about the current state of affairs:

> In more than 40 nations around the world today Christians are being persecuted for their faith. In some of these nations it is illegal to own a Bible, to share your faith in Christ, change your faith or teach your children about Jesus. Those who boldly follow Christ—in spite of government edict or radical opposition—can face harassment, arrest, torture, and even death. Yet Christians continue to meet for worship and to witness for Christ, and the church in restricted nations is growing.[12]

This widespread persecution results in thousands of believers imprisoned for their faith. Paul says that we are to remember brothers and sisters in chains, "as if chained with them" (Hebrews 13:3). You can become an advocate for imprisoned Christians around the world by:

- Praying for the persecuted and imprisioned Christians around the world
- Writing words of encouragement to let them know they are not forgotten
- Contacting government officials to ask for their release
- Giving money to support the prisoner's families, often left with few resources and barely able to survive

Visit www.prisoneralert.com to find many practical ways to become an advocate for those imprisoned for their faith.

You can also reach out to prisoners in the United States. Often these men and women have come to the end of their rope and are eager and willing to receive the message of the Gospel. They need a listening ear, a word of encouragement, and to know that hope is not lost for them. Learn more about prison ministry in your area by visiting the following websites: www.prisonfellowship.org and www.prisonministry.net.

The Sick

> *I was sick and you visited Me.*
> (MATTHEW 25:36)

One of the most forgotten groups of people in our country are the elderly, who are often left to spend the final years of their lives alone in a nursing home, wasting away the hours in front of the television. Local nursing homes are delighted to have volunteers visit the residents, talk with them, read to them, or play games with them. Just spending a few hours a week can bring much-needed light into their lives. And what a great opportunity to witness to them about the hope of eternity in the final weeks, months, or years of their lives.

Local communities often have homes and organizations for disabled people. Volunteer to be a friend to a disabled person. Take them on outings or just get together and let them know they have value.

Local hospitals are thankful for volunteers who will come and sing, read, or visit with the patients. My brothers and I used to sing once a week at a hospital for terminally ill respiratory patients, and just spending a few minutes in their rooms with a guitar brought amazing joy to their lives. It opened the door for us to share the Gospel with many of them. We even spent Christmas Day one year visiting the patients, singing Christmas carols and reading the Christmas story—and it was probably the best Christmas we ever had.

The Foreigner

> *I was a stranger and you took Me in.*
> (MATTHEW 25:35)

There are 14,047,300 men, women, and children in the world today forced to be refugees—displaced, impoverished, their very lives endangered. Hundreds of thousands flee to the U.S. for safety.[13] Sadly, many face a bleak reality once they are here. Without language, skills, or resources, they struggle to make ends meet, and many are unable to get their feet under them. They are required to apply for immigration within the first year of being in the U.S., but few of them have the knowledge or skills to go through the process. Refugees in the United States are the ultimate example of the "stranger in the land" that God refers to all throughout Scripture, asking us to remember them and meet their needs. Refugees are in desperate need of practical assistance, encouragement, and support. For a more complete look at the issues refugees are facing, visit www.refugees.org, or www.unhcr.org.

Every city in America that hosts refugees has a refugee resettlement service. Do a quick Google search to find out information about one near you, contact them, and ask how you can get involved. This agency can also direct you to other organizations working with refugees.

More than anything, refugees who have come to America need mentors who will take a personal interest in them. Consider "adopting" a refugee family in your local city and take them grocery shopping, to doctor's appointments, and visit their homes to help them set up a checkbook, help them understand their mail, etc. Refugees come from fleeing genocide in many circumstances to getting thrown into a refugee camp where they live in utter poverty and desolation. Coming to America causes drastic culture shock, which causes high percentages of depression and mental illness as well as homelessness. When a relationship is established with refugees, it provides incredible hope and stability, and gives you a great opportunity to share the Gospel.

The Privilege of Pouring Out

A sacred opportunity awaits you. We have the privilege of pouring out our lives for others, just as Christ did for us. If you have entered into a covenant with the King of all kings, then this life is no longer about you. Your body is meant to be a living sacrifice for Him. As it says in Ephesians 2:10, "We are His workmanship, created in Christ Jesus for good works, which God prepared beforehand that we should walk in them." God has an amazing work prepared for you. And when you begin taking steps toward serving the least, and prayerfully seeking His guidance and direction, He will be more than faithful to show you what, where, when, how, and who you are meant to serve. Remember, you don't need to be superqualified or have everything figured out ahead of time. You just need a heart fully surrendered to the One who does.

Final Thoughts

*This I say, brethren, the time is short, so that from now on even
those who have wives should be as though they had none.*
1 Corinthians 7:29

*No one engaged in warfare entangles himself with the affairs of
this life, that he may please Him who enlisted him as a soldier.*
2 Timothy 2:4

My precious sisters, we are not in a time of peace. We are in a time of war.

The battle of the ages is about to begin. Death and life hang in the balance for millions. Out of the ashes of dead religion a struggle has been born between truth and deception that will alter the church forever. To the victor go the spoils. By God's grace we must do everything in our power to see living, vibrant, and relevant historic Christianity rise from this conflict as the emergent victor to represent Jesus Christ for the next century and beyond, with love, honor, and power.

We must remember that we are soldiers of the cross, whether single or married. This life is but a fleeing breath. Singleness is a short season. Marriage is a short season. Heaven is for eternity.

As Paul says, even those of us with spouses are to be so committed to Christ that He is all that matters. Sisters, let us not get caught up in the affairs of this life. Singleness, marriage, and romance— yes, these things are important to God. Yes, He cares very deeply about them. *But that's not what life is all about.*

Last year a young woman I knew well, Kate, was preparing to be married to her high school sweetheart. A few months before the wedding, she went to see the movie *The End of the Spear*, which portrayed the true story of Nate Saint, Jim Elliot, and other young missionaries to Ecuador who were martyred for their faith in Christ. The story had a deep impact upon Kate. She told me, "As much as I love Matt and am excited to be getting married to him, I can't build my life around him. I must surrender him daily to Christ. If God chooses to take him home, I have to be willing to relinquish him. Matt can't be the one I lean on; it has to be God alone. I realize that now more than ever."

This is what Paul meant when he said we are to live as if we do not have spouses. It's what Christ meant when He said we must forsake father, mother, spouse, and all that we have for His sake. Let us not forget the countless men and women throughout all the ages that have sacrificed those they loved for the cause of Christ. If they have willingly laid down everything, can we not willingly lay down our own dreams to become a consecrated soldier for our King?

Let us never forget that He is worthy.

Bonus Section

An Interview with Krissy on Radiant Singleness

Throughout this book you have heard me talk about Krissy, my beautiful sister-in-law who lived as a radiant, purpose-filled single woman until the age of 34. She lived out one of the best examples of Christ-centered singleness I've ever seen. A few nights ago I called her and asked if I could interview her for this book. She graciously complied. Following is our conversation. I hope you'll be blessed and inspired by all that she shared with me!

Leslie: Krissy, I know that you were set apart for Christ from a very young age. Do you remember when He begin to draw your heart?

Krissy: Oh, yes! I remember it very clearly, even though I was only six years old at the time. My family moved around *a lot* when I was little. I remember experiencing loneliness and fear, being thrust into new situations all the time. But I was really aware that God was there, and that He saw me. I wanted to know Him. If you can believe it, I was about six when I first felt the Holy Spirit work in my heart, causing me to understand that I carried a burden of sin and guilt and that I didn't have the power to live a good and godly life on my own; that I needed His power to work in me. I guess that was when I surrendered my life to Jesus. And I remember feeling so happy and joyful!

When I was in high school, I wasn't popular or social. I guess you would have called me a wallflower. In my senior yearbook, I was voted "Most Quiet," which really wasn't a compliment! I didn't have many friends, but this was the season in which I really drew close to God as never before. I developed a deep hunger and craving for His Word. He spoke to me in an intimate and personal way through the Scriptures. I took a lot of walks, praying, meditating on His Word, speaking Scripture, worshipping, and making up songs of praise to Him. Jesus was my close Friend.

Leslie: Wow. That's beautiful! He used that lonely time to call you away with Him! So tell me about your single years, and how God used your life for His kingdom.

Krissy: I remember one day after I graduated from high school that God really began speaking to me about taking risks. I realized that my name, "Kris," held the same letters as the word "Risk." But I was the last person in the world to take risks! God wanted me to get out of my comfort zone. I began to experience God speaking to me very specifically about my calling, giving me promises, especially in areas where I felt extremely weak. In things I didn't feel qualified to do, God showed me through His Word that my weaknesses weren't a problem for Him. It wasn't about my weakness, but about His strength.

Leslie: Amen to that! So how did you figure out what kind of risks He wanted you to take?

Krissy: One day I just said to God, "What do You want to do with my life? Where do You want to take me?" I felt Him speak to me from Psalm 45:10-11: "Listen, O daughter, consider and give ear: the king is enthralled by your beauty" (NIV). I felt those verses were His heart for me, and I remember thinking, "Beauty? What beauty?" But God saw something beautiful that He wanted to work *in* me. I felt clearly that He was calling me apart from my family, away from everything that I knew, to offer Him my life.

Leslie: That must have been scary for a shy 18-year-old girl! Where did you end up going?

Krissy: He took me into places I never would have naturally gone. I did mission work in inner-cities in Mexico, New Orleans, and Chicago. In those situations I really began feeling His heart, hearing His voice, experiencing His amazing grace working through me to speak boldly into people's lives, and I knew it wasn't me; it was Him. That was when I really saw the power of the Gospel to save. I knew I was witnessing something much greater than myself, something beyond me.

Later God led me to Romania, where I lived in an orphanage with 90 young girls. When I saw how these girls had been abandoned by everyone they had ever known, I was rather angry with the Lord that He would bring me into this place, knowing I could not stay forever. I was afraid I would just become one more abandonment in these girls' lives. But one night God came and revealed His amazing Father's heart to us through a married couple that had both lost their fathers as young ages. They shared how God had been a Father to them. God showed up that night and revealed Himself as an intimate Father to these girls. When the time came for me to leave them, they were the ones comforting me! They said, "It's okay, you can go. Our Father is with us!" Even when they would write me letters, they were always talking about the Father and how He was with them. I will never forget that, knowing we are simply called to obey Him and we will see Him reveal Himself.

I felt so little and helpless to make a difference in those girls' lives. But I began to pray Psalm 68 for them; that He would lead the prisoners out with singing and set the solitary in families. I prayed that every one of those orphans would find a home. And years later I began meeting those girls in the United States who had been adopted into families. I ran into five different girls from that orphanage! One of them actually ended up right down the road from me in Michigan! God hears and answers prayer.

Leslie: Okay, here is the million dollar question…How did you walk through so many years of singleness with so much joy? How did you stay content, even though you desired to be married and have children?

Krissy: It wasn't easy! I continually had to surrender my desires to God. There were times that I felt really, really lonely. And I thought, "Jesus, You were lonely when You walked this earth; when You walked the road of Calvary. If this is one small way that I can identify with You in Your sufferings—I rejoice. I want to know You and draw closer to You through this. I know I won't have an opportunity like this again."

When I was single, I had to surrender my hopes of marriage. But once I got married, I had to surrender my singleness! It was a gift, an opportunity, and amazing privilege to walk so intimately and lean so much on Jesus during my single years. I had been single for so long, it wasn't so easy to let go of it.

Leslie: What do you think was God's purpose in having you wait so long for your husband?

Krissy: Those years as a single young women were crucial for my growth, my foundation. It would have been very easy for me to just find a man and hide in him instead of really having to become the person God created me to be. I had to learn how to hide in Jesus; how to lean all my weight on Him. I needed to learn how to communicate. I needed to blossom in Him. My single years were critical for Him shaping me into who I am today.

Leslie: I observed you closely during your twenties, and your intimate love relationship with Christ really blessed and inspired me. What helped you cultivate that kind of intimacy with Christ, and how would you encourage other young women to do the same?

Krissy: Take time to *listen* to Him every day, even if it seems like a foolish thing to do. Ask Him specific questions. Wait for Him, and He will speak. I love John 10:27, which says, "My sheep hear My voice, and I know them, and they follow Me." That is one of the most powerful Scriptures. God knowing us, and us knowing God. When we know Him, we can't help but follow Him, and when we do we will follow Him into places we never dreamed we could go. That's what will change the world; when people see that we have been with Jesus. Don't miss the opportunity to build intimacy with Christ when you are single! Marriage and family are a transition. It's harder to keep your intimacy with Christ at the forefront because there are a lot of other things pulling at your attention. I am so grateful I built a foundation of intimacy with Christ during my single years, because I have to work extra hard to find that intimacy with Him now that I am a wife and mother. I would also encourage my single sisters to read some of the books that greatly impacted me during those years: Gladys Aylward's story, Amy Carmichael's story, and two others that l love: *Anointed for Burial* and *Of Whom the World Was Not Worthy*. These are stories of women and how God worked dramatically in their lives.

Leslie: Great advice! So, was it hard to wait for God's perfect timing?

Krissy: Yes! It was the hardest thing I have ever had to do. In my early thirties, I was living in rural Michigan. I was around young children and families, but no available young men were around at all. It didn't seem like a very wise place to claim my man. There was plenty of pressure all around me to take matters into my own hands. I had people wanting to set me up and people telling me to move somewhere else where there would be more available men. I remember reading Proverbs 18:22, which says that a man who finds a wife, finds a good thing. I recognized that the man is the one who does the finding. And I thought, "Well, my man will have to come and find me. God knows where I am. God can show him where I am."

Romans 8:32 was also a great comfort to me: "He who did not spare His own Son, but delivered Him up for us all, how shall He not with Him also freely give us all things?" But even so, my faith was stretched to the limit. It seemed that just before God brought Scott into my life, my desire to be married became overwhelmingly intense. I would weep with longing for a companion. I had prayed for my husband for years, but I felt spiritually exhausted, and that I was losing my strength to keep praying for him. Right at that point, God brought Scott to me. He had put that desire in my heart so that He could fulfill it.

Leslie: What has been your greatest joy in seeing God's faithfulness in this area of your life?

Krissy: My greatest joy is being on this journey with my King. "Eye has not seen, nor ear heard, nor have entered into the heart of man the things which God has prepared for those who love Him," says 1 Corinthians 2:9. I am on a journey with my husband and kids, and I know God will lead us step by step. I tell Scotty and my kids all the time how many years I longed for them and prayed for them—and how they are God's answer to my heart's desire. He is faithful!

Notes

Chapter 1—Forsaking All

1. Elisabeth Elliot, *Quest for Love* (Tarrytown, NY: Fleming H. Revell Company, 2002), 40.
2. Corrie ten Boom, *Each New Day* (Tarrytown, NY: Fleming H. Revell Company, 2003), 69.

Chapter 2—The Pattern of True Christianity

Epigraph: Amy Carmichael, *Gold Cord* (Fort Washington, PA: CLC Publications, 1991), 68. Used by permission.

1. Elisabeth Elliot, *Passion and Purity* (Tarrytown, NY: Fleming H. Revell Company, 2002).
2. Oswald Chambers, *Abandoned to God* (Grand Rapids, MI: Discovery House Publishers, 1998), 143.
3. Norman Grubb, *Rees Howells: Intercessor* (Fort Washington, PA: Christian Literature Crusade, 1952), 141.
4. Paris Reidhead, "Ten Shekels and a Shirt," www.sermonindex.com.
5. Hannah Hurnard, *Hind's Feet on High Places* (Wheaton, IL: Tyndale, 1997), 294.
6. Elisabeth Elliot, *Quest for Love*, 38.

Chapter 3—Finding Romantic Fulfillment

Epigraph: Elisabeth Elliot, *Quest for Love*, 163.

1. Leslie Ludy, *Authentic Beauty* (Colorado Springs, CO: Multnomah, 2007), 32.
2. Corrie ten Boom, *Tramp for the Lord* (Fort Washington, PA: Christian Literature Crusade, 2008), 160.
3. Trevor Yaxley, *William and Catherine* (Grand Rapids, MI: Bethany House, 2003), 65.
4. Jeanne Guyon, *Experiencing the Depths of Christ* (Grand Rapids, MI: Bethany House, 2003), 35.

Chapter 4—The Modern Church and Singleness

1. Debbie Maken, *Getting Serious About Getting Married: Rethinking the Gift of Singleness* (Wheaton, IL: Crossway Books, 2006), 43.
2. Ibid., 28.
3. Candice Watters, *Get Married: What Women Can Do to Help it Happen* (Chicago, IL: Moody Publishers, 2008), 22, 28.

Chapter 5—Contentment in Christ

1. Candice Watters, *Get Married*, 22.
2. Leslie Ludy, *Set-Apart Femininity* (Eugene, OR: Harvest House Publishers, 2008), 134-35.
3. Charles Spurgeon, *A Good Soldier of Christ*, page 3, Sermon 938, spurgeongems.org.

Chapter 6—Giving God a Hand

1. Debbie Maken, *Getting Serious About Getting Married*, 140.
2. Candice Watters, *Get Married*, 19.
3. Ian Thomas, *Indwelling Life*, (Sisters, OR: Multnomah, 2006), 20.

4. Elisabeth Elliot, *Passion and Purity*, 100.
5. Candice Watters, *Get Married*, 114.
6. Ibid.
7. Ibid.
8. Dake's Annotated Reference Bible (Lawrenceville, GA: Dake Bible Sales, Inc, 1989), 293.
9. Ibid.

Chapter 7—Marriage Above All Else

1. Candice Watters, *Get Married*, 47.
2. Ibid., 48.
3. G.D. Watson, *Others May, You Cannot* (from Faith, Prayer, & Tract League: Tract #76; Grand Rapids, MI).
4. Elisabeth Elliot, *Passion and Purity*, 68.
5. Hannah Whitehall Smith, quoted in Elisabeth Elliot, *Quest for Love*, 39.

Chapter 8—Doesn't God Want Me to Be Happy?

Epigraph: Elisabeth Elliot, *Passion and Purity*, 44.
1. Debbie Maken, *Getting Serious About Getting Married*, back cover and 28.
2. Ibid., 105-106.

Chapter 9—The Sacred Opportunity of Singleness

1. Derek and Lydia Prince, *Appointment in Jerusalem* (North Kensington, PA: Whitaker House, 2005), 9-10.
2. Leslie Ludy, *Set-Apart Femininity*, 201.

Chapter 11—Getting Started Changing the World

1. *Ten Ways Every Christian Can Care for the Orphan and Waiting Child*, free brochure by Family Life Today, Little Rock, AK (order brochure at store.familylife.com).
2. Vernon Brewer, WorldHelp.net.
3. Norman Grubb, *Rees Howells: Intercessor*, 92.
4. www.cryoftheorphan.org/Display.asp?Page=WhatHappens.
5. *Ten Ways Every Christian Can Care for the Orphan and Waiting Child*, free brochure by Family Life Today, Little Rock, AK.
6. Danita Estrella, quote taken from www.danitaschildren.org.
7. montevideo.usembassy.gov/usaweb/2008/08-537EN.shtml.
8. Rita Springer, quoted in Natalie Nichols Gillespie, *Successful Adoption: A Guide for Christian Families* (Nashville, TN: Integrity Publishers, 2006), 239-40.
9. www.cryoftheorphan.org/Display.asp?Page=WhatHappens.
10. Quote from "What Is Human Trafficking?" www.salvationarmyusa.org.
11. State Department statistics, www.ucountcampaign.org.
12. Voice of the Martyrs, www.prisoneralert.com/vompw_persecution.htm.
13. www.refugees.org/article.aspx?id=2186&subm=33&ssm=36&area=Investigate.

Looking for ways to live a
set-apart life for Christ?

www.setapart(girl).com

Leslie Ludy's Online Living Room

Living as a set-apart young woman in
today's world is not easy.

I invite you to visit setapartgirl.com
for encouragement, inspiration, and
fellowship with other like-minded
young women.

Setapartgirl.com is my way of con-
necting with you, cheering you on,
and providing you with the tools
you need to live this message out on
a day-to-day, moment-by-moment
basis. You'll find blogs, articles, in-
terviews, podcasts, event info, and
lots of peeks into my life, family,
and daily walk with Christ.

Hope to see you there!

Leslie Ludy

Other Books by Leslie Ludy

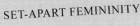

a message from Leslie:

SET-APART FEMININITY

Do you long for something more than the shallow, self-focused, pleasure-seeking femininity so prevalent today? Do you want a focus beyond chasing male approval and pop-culture appeal? Do you need a fresh vision of God's amazing purpose for your life as a young woman? Are you ready to become one of the few in this generation who will make an eternal impact upon this world?

Discover set-apart femininity. This is a powerful, candid, conversational book in which I pass on a compelling vision for femininity that can forever alter your existence and take you far beyond the unfulfilling trends of modern culture. This book is not the same old mediocre message you've always heard. It's a radical call to a countercultural lifestyle in which every aspect of your femininity—from the way you relate with guys to the focus and direction of your life—is shaped by an intimate relationship with the King of kings. It's the kind of heroic femininity that the world-changing women of history understood. And it's well within your grasp, no matter where you've been.

ANSWERING THE GUY QUESTIONS

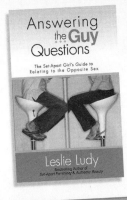

Answering the Guy Questions tackles some of the toughest questions I get asked about guy/girl relationships. It is very specific and practical and helps you apply the set-apart lifestyle to the often confusing area of guys. It also addresses the issue of modern male mediocrity—it will give you a vision for how you can help the guys in your life experience true manhood as God intended it to be, in all of its glory, strength, nobility, and honor. If you have ever been discouraged, disgusted, depressed, or even defeated by the state of modern guys, this book can infuse you with vision, hope, and a practical means of doing something about it! I also love that this book is short and to the point—a very easy read if you don't have a lot of time!

To learn more about Harvest House books and
to read sample chapters, log on to our website:

www.harvesthousepublishers.com

HARVEST HOUSE PUBLISHERS
EUGENE, OREGON